Life Is Short Then You're Dead Forever

A Realistic Self-Help Book

L.A. Nik™

The author and publisher specifically disclaim all responsibility for any liability, loss, or risk (personal or otherwise) which is incurred as a result (directly or indirectly) of the use of the contents of this book.

ISBN-13: 978-0-9887898-0-7

To all the big dreamers and believers who make shit happen.

Acknowledgements

John P. Goetz – Writer

Kristen Kuehn - Contributing Writer

Special thanks to Bank at the Westin Minneapolis

Cover designed by Rock Star Services LLC

Cover photos by Nancy Kuehn Photography

CHAPTER 1

INTRODUCTION

I've known of too many people (and have talked to thousands) who are simply not living. They think they are but they're not. They're treading water at best. Most are stuck in loveless marriages. They are stuck in the corporate rut – wearing the same suit day after day, riding the same elevator to the office but going nowhere. They take the same freeway, subway, or train day after day. They all have a mortgage with a picket fence. Two cars. Two kids. A cat. A dog. They are doing what their parents, family, and society expect.

They think they are living the American dream.

The problem is that it's more of a nightmare than any dream.

They just don't know how to wake up.

When you are on your deathbed recounting your life, are you going to be like the majority of people and think, "I'm glad this ride is over with"? Or do you want to be able to say, "That was bad ass! I want to do that again!"

After reading this book, I want you to be learn to live life to the fullest and understand that, "Life is Short and Then You're Dead Forever."

There are no second chances.

No do-overs.

You can't get on the ride again once it's over with.

When you're dead, you're dead.

Forever.

And, like most of us, you'll be forgotten in two or three generations.

I know that sounds depressing but you know it's true. There are very few who even know the names of their great-grandparents. Odds are that your great-grandchildren won't know your name either. So, instead of living life with dread, waiting for it to end, wouldn't it be better to live your life like you're on the best roller coaster ride you've ever ridden instead of treating life like an IRS audit the rest of your life?

This isn't your typical self-help book. Unlike most others you will find or may have already read and that are now probably used to level your kitchen table, this one is *realistic* - not fluffy. It's realistic in that it's one born from my personal experiences and mistakes I've made. You will not find any feathery prose or poetry. There are no biblical passages. There are no tapes to buy. No chants to memorize. Everyone can learn to steer their lives in the right direction. Everyone can learn to love life the way I do.

It is just realistic, straight-forward advice on how to live your life without regret.

Advice on how to pull yourself out of the fifteen-year rut that most middle-age people find themselves stuck in and unable to move..

If you are young enough, perhaps you will learn what mistakes *not* to make in the first place.

This book explains how you can live your life each and every day.

There are nine more chapters in this book. Each one builds on the other. Each one discusses the three basic building blocks every person needs to live life to its fullest. Each and everyone one of us needs to *Learn*, *Create*, and *Share*. If you are not doing these on a daily basis, you are not living.

Chapter 2: The Power of Confidence

Look at yourself in the mirror. Do you like what you see? You have to get the confidence to shout your name from the rooftops. The Power of Confidence is the cornerstone of everything.

Chapter 3: The Power of Difference

Your only value in life is how you differ from everyone else. You need to show the world how different you are and how you're unique. Look at a carton of eggs, does any one egg stand out from the rest? No! Now take one out, replace it with a brown one, and look at the carton of eggs again.

Chapter 4: The Power of Place

Don't just maintain your life. Live your life. The Power of Place is essential for the evolution of *you*. Along with Confidence and Difference, it's another vital building block in your growth. Learn to diversify – to expand beyond your home, your hometown, even beyond your family and friends.

Chapter 5: The Power of Finesse

It's not what you say; it's how you say it. If the Power of Place is an essential building block for the evolution of "you," then The Power of Finesse is an essential building block for the evolution of your relationships and daily life. Finesse is key for every relationship – your mate, your boss, your co-workers.

Chapter 6: The Power of Communication

Don't just talk. Communicate. The Power of Communication, like Finesse, is learned. You are not born with it and, like most lessons in this book, it's acquired through experience. Communication is a combination of confidence and finesse and once you have it, the world can be yours.

Chapter 7: The Power of Responsibility

Life is short. Why make it shorter? None of us are worth anything without others. We have to respect and care for others in our lives in order to fulfill our own. Everything we do has a consequence that can affect others either in a positive or negative way.

Chapter 8: The Comfortable State of Hatred

Be careful what you wish for, you just might get it. Everyone has told you that in order to be truly happy, you had to get that job. To get that house. To get married. To have three kids. To have a riding lawnmower. To buy a minivan for your wife and a Range Rover for yourself. To have a housekeeper come twice a week to clean your five-bedroom, four thousand square foot home. Now that you have it, do you feel any better?

Chapter 9: The Power of Persistence

Don't lie to promote yourself. Exaggerate. When you want something to happen, make it happen. But you can't do it all alone. Nobody can. You have to associate with people who have confidence in you and support your dreams and your ideas. Those people are out there – it's up to you to get out and find them.

Chapter 10: The Power of Dreams

If you don't have dreams, you can't be living. Underlining everything in life are your dreams. Too many people have stopped believing in themselves. They're stuck in that comfortable state of hatred and they are watching time (and their dreams) slip by. Don't let this happen to you.

CHAPTER 2

THE POWER OF CONFIDENCE

Shout your name from the rooftops!

Look at yourself in the mirror. Do you like what you see?

I'm not talking about whether you're short, fat, tall, or skinny. Confidence has nothing to do with appearance. I'm talking about, do you like "YOU!" If you can't look at yourself in the mirror and smile back at yourself, you are missing a critical building block to life – the key building block for success. It's the most important component of this book.

Confidence.

Without confidence you might as well get off the ride right now.

I have confidence – I know it. I didn't always. But I do now – and it shows in everything I do, everyplace I go, and everyone I meet. When I walk into a room, people see someone with his head held high, who's making direct eye contact, and who isn't afraid to say "Hi. I'm Nik." When I walk into a room, people think, "Wow. Who's that?" People can feel my confidence. You will never see me walking into a room, cowering in a corner trying to be invisible.

I *want* to be noticed.

I have the confidence to get things done and get what I want out of life. It's that simple. Don't misunderstand. I'm not cocky. I'm confident. There's a difference.

"Cocky" is the high school football player or cheerleader who thinks they are owed something. They are cocky because they've been put on a pedestal that is meaningless. "Cocky" is the executive who ridicules employees because he or she is really afraid. A person is cocky because they've been *told* they were better than everyone else. When I encounter someone who is cocky, I just laugh as I know that he will eventually fall flat on his face. It's true. I see it happen every day.

"Confidence," on the other hand, is not given to you. You earn it. You learn it. It's knowing that you are essentially good. That you provide value. That your opinion counts. That you are worth the raise you are asking for. There's a fine line between cockiness and confidence. The confident person can be the squeaky wheel, is intelligent enough to know when to stop squeaking, and eventually gets what he wants – a raise, for example. The cocky person squeaks until he's fired – because he thinks he *owed* the raise.

Have you ever created something that you were proud of but were too scared and insecure to tell anyone about? I know hundreds of song writers who possess incredible talent but lack the confidence to say, "I wrote this and it's fucking good."

I'll say something like, "Hey, that's a great song! Have you let anyone else hear that?"

The guy will look down at the floor, shake his head, and say, "No. I couldn't do that."

The song is stuck in a drawer never to see the light of day. People without confidence? They are just like the song - they are stuck too. They are stuck in a corporate rut, riding the same elevator to their cubicle, hoping for a raise and not getting one. Their dream, their real talent, is stuck in the same drawer with the song. When you have done something that you are proud of, let the world know. Let your boss know. Let your family know. Let your mate know.

Shout it from the rooftops!

Let the world know what you've done.

Be confident.

Everything in life, everything you do, every person you want to meet, starts with having confidence in yourself and knowing who you are.

Who you honestly are.

Be yourself. Never play dress-up.

*

The seed of confidence is planted when you are young. It's up to you to let it grow. Think back to when you were in grade school. You learned 2 + 2 = 4. It was a fact and you knew it. And when the teacher asked the class what the answer to 2 + 2 was, you raised your hand because you were confident and you absolutely knew you were right. No one could tell you 2 + 2 = 5.

Think about how you felt on the inside at that moment. That feeling of knowing what's true and the confidence you felt about knowing it.

That's the kind of confidence I have every day. I know myself inside and out. I know what

I'm capable of. I know what I'm good at and where I have talent. I also know what I'm not good at. I also don't care about what I'm not good at. I can get other people to do those things for me.

As can you.

That's the Power of Confidence. That's where it all starts.

*

When and where did I gain my confidence?

I became me in 9th grade. I opened my eyes and everything just looked different. The sky looked different. I looked different in the mirror. I can't explain it, but that day when I looked in the mirror, it was the first time I liked what I saw. My confidence had taken root.

Up until that day, I was very insecure. My hair was wild and everybody tried to tame it. My mom, my grandma, my teachers – they all tried to part it and make it lay down, but it wouldn't. It didn't matter what they did or whatever goop they put in my hair, it just did its own thing. So eventually I said, "Fuck it" and just went with it.

Nothing worked for me before that day. Nothing was like how I wanted it. I didn't get the respect I wanted. I wasn't comfortable in my own skin. I didn't look the way I wanted. I didn't have the friends I wanted. I couldn't say what I wanted to say. I was little. I was skinny. My hair looked ridiculous. Nothing worked.

The summer between 8th and 9th grade I was starting to discover myself. So when I started school in the 9th grade, I was *the* guy. Did you ever see that "Hot for Teacher" video by Van Halen? Remember the nerdy kid with the glasses and greasy hair?

That was me!

I left 8th grade as the dorky little nerd that nobody knew and came back as a Rock Star and everyone wanted to be my friend.

I can't explain it and I don't know how to teach someone to have the same experience I had. But have you ever just *known* something good was going to happen? You knew you were going to get the job, ace the test, or even get the girl. That was the feeling I had that morning. Except it wasn't about one thing in particular - it was an overall feeling of knowing myself and that I felt confident about whatever it was I was putting out there.

On the flip side, everyone knows when something bad is going to happen too. Did you ever go to school and forgot your homework? You knew you were going to get in trouble for it. Why can't we do the same thing but only believe that something good is going to happen? If we accept that bad things are going to happen in life beyond our control, then shouldn't we be confident in ourselves and the things we can control?

Confidence means embracing who you *really* are and freely expressing that to the world.

People need to embrace those moments when they feel proud of their accomplishments. Ever have that feeling when you've worked hard on something and you know you did a great job and you have that sense of pride? That's what I'm talking about! We all need that! You have to know where your strengths are and nobody can do that for you.

You control your destiny.

Confidence helps you get there faster.

When you've accomplished something on your own, you know it's good, then you feel on top of the world. You feel confident and it shows. It shows in your attitude, the way you walk, the way you approach people, the way you talk. It's infectious. People want to be around that. They're drawn to it. They want to be you and learn from you.

Most people will have this feeling for a few days after they've accomplished something. My challenge to you is to hold onto that feeling for the rest of your life. Take that which you know is right about yourself and hold onto it. Never let it go. So no matter what comes your way in life you can always bank on that and know.

I have my days where I'm down. Everybody has those days. But I still like myself and I like who I am down deep. I may not have liked who I had become for awhile but even then, I still remembered who I was and I liked that part of me.

I like who I am and it doesn't matter to me if anyone else does. I have to live with me.

They don't.

Even with people I deal with professionally. If I don't like what they want to do, I'll stay true to myself and do it my way. I always have. I don't care if someone else is an "expert" at something. I still want it done my way and it is my decision whether to work with them or not. Learn to walk away. You do not owe anyone anything.

I don't have all the answers. I've gotten a lot of help from people along the way. I've allowed people to help me. I've let people present their ideas to me. But all these things I've allowed in my life never stopped or hindered me from still being myself. None of these people or ideas tried to change who I was. If anything, they helped me become more of what I already was.

*

Your confidence needs fertilizer to grow. Give yourself achievable goals and believe me, your confidence will grow like mine did.

It's true!

When I was in 7th or 8th grade, I was miserable. I thought to myself, "I would sell myself to the devil to make it in the music business."

So then I started to make a wish whenever I had to pee.

It was a simple, achievable goal.

In the school's bathroom urinals, they had those vinyl screens with the holes over the drain. I would aim through the hole. I was sure that the longer I could pee in the hole, the more my wish was going to come true. I made it a game and did this each time I went.

I wished I was cooler.

I wished girls would like me.

I wished to be a rock star.

I wished people would leave me the fuck alone and just let me do my thing.

The night before I became me, I peed in that hole perfectly. Best time ever. Every drop went in that hole. When I woke up the morning after the perfect pee, everything was different. Since that day, no one ever picked on me again. The teachers treated me differently. The other students left me alone. And if something did happen, the jocks would stick up for me. I suddenly became cool – overnight. All the teachers were rooting for me.

Suddenly, everyone was on my side - even my parents.

My pee-in-the-hole goal worked.

For me at least.

You might need to try something different.

Of course now I know there's no magic when you pee in a hole. But the fact is, I did believe it would work. I convinced myself. I truly believed that my life would change and it did.

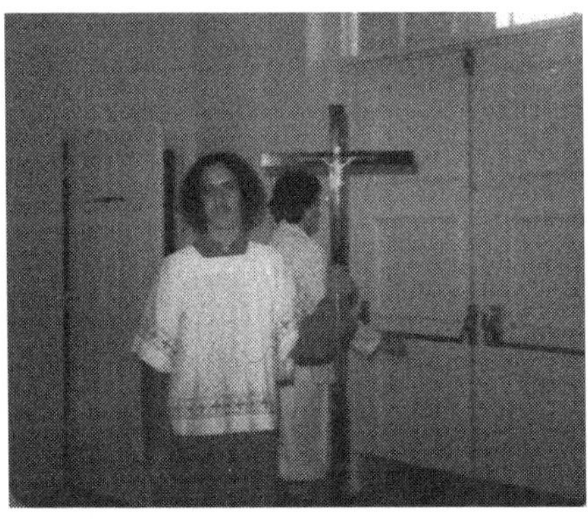

Left: I looked in the mirror and felt awkward.
Right: I looked in the mirror and felt confident!

The biggest obstacle you will ever have to face in life is yourself and your own insecurities. If you can get past yourself, and be confident in who you really are inside, you will be the success you were meant to be.

You have to believe in yourself and your own power. You have to know yourself and show that confidence everywhere you go. There is nothing else you can do right now to improve your life until you have the confidence you can do it first. I've known people who get success and wealth too early and they fuck it up. They didn't have the confidence to take their life to the next step. They didn't have enough confidence to learn, create, and share.

*

Why do you think there are so many one hit wonders in the music industry? Because most of those hits were complete flukes!

Why couldn't they continue their success?

They became cocky – not confident.

They didn't *learn*.

Even the musicians are usually surprised when they get a hit and they don't have the confidence in their own abilities and talents to make another one. So they break up, develop a drug habit, spend all their money, and end up working at a grocery store. They didn't learn anything from their single success. They let the temporary fame bring them down.

I've seen it so many times.

Those who made it past the first single nurtured their confidence. They learned to improve their musical talent.

The learned to *create*.

Look at the successful bands that put out lots of hits. They fill stadiums. They know they are good. They know they have talent. Not because someone told them, or they thought the audience owed them applause, but because of the confidence each band member had in his individual talent.

Ultimately, they learned to share. They knew they had something to share with an audience and they put in their time and struggled until they finally get a deal. But it all started with confidence. They had to believe it was going to happen - no matter what.

The point I'm trying to make is you have to believe in yourself. I didn't work hard to discover myself, I didn't go on a journey to "find" myself, it just happened. But once I knew who I was, I was treated differently. I saw it for myself and I've seen it in others.

*

I call this inherent feeling of confidence, the "It Factor." Not everyone is going to be a rock star. But you can have "It" in whatever industry you want to be in. You can be a rock star bartender. You can be a rock star parent. You can be a rock star investment banker. You can be a rock star in your life. Just remember to learn, create, and share each and every day.

Not everybody has "It."

"It" is you.

The *real* you.

It's knowing who you really are. No one can shake it from you. No one can take it away from you. When you honestly know who you are and what you're made of, you have "It."

I've been to the Oscars and I've been to several after-parties. I've seen some of these celebrities on TV and I think to myself, "How the hell did they make it? They're not that great. I don't get it. How'd they become famous?"

I watch very little TV, but I remember many actresses I have watched. I remember one in particular – let's call her Sue. I didn't get it when I saw her on TV. I didn't think she was that attractive. I didn't think she was funny or that great of an actress. I didn't understand why people were making such a big deal about her for or why she was even famous.

But then I saw her walk into the room at the Oscars party and I knew instantly why. She had "It." When she walked in, everybody noticed and everybody's jaw dropped, including mine. She had that confidence. She talked to anyone and everyone. She owned that room! After meeting her in person, I understood the appeal.

When you meet these people in person you realize why they're famous. It's not their talent. Lots of famous people have no talent at all. But they do have confidence. They all have that "thing" that makes people notice them. They get noticed and that's what gets you famous.

Think of it this way. Have you ever been out to a dance club and you see some hot chick on the dance floor with some tight fitting dress on with her chest hanging out but she's looking all around her and constantly adjusting herself. She's not smiling and she's barely moving. Then, on the other side of the dance floor, there's a heavier woman that's dancing and laughing and looking like she's having the time of her life? Who are you going to want to hang out with? Who's going to be more fun? The one with the confidence!

Like I said, confidence has nothing to do with appearance. Confidence has everything to do with "It."

Just because some chick slaps on some skanky outfit doesn't mean she has the confidence to pull it off. If how you look on the outside isn't reflecting how you feel about yourself on the inside, it's going to show!

Confidence is not acting.

Confidence is being comfortable with who you are – inside and out.

If you're uncomfortable with what you're wearing, people will notice! You'll be far sexier wearing something that you feel comfortable and confident in than in something you're going to be self conscious about all night.

Nothing is hotter than a chick with real confidence. If you don't have confidence underneath the wrapping paper, no one is going to treat you like a gift.

When you have confidence, you stand out. Nobody makes fun of the insecure wallflower because nobody knows they're there! Bullies never pick on those who are confident and secure in themselves. Well, they might try. But if you have confidence in yourself, you won't even notice them trying to pick on you. You won't hear them. You won't see them. You won't know they exist.

Don't get me wrong, people with confidence will have haters. I have lots of haters! I'm proud of it! It means I'm getting attention! Haters are simply people without confidence. They are jealous because you have "It."

Celebrities deal with this on a daily basis. There are magazines and blogs devoted to hating them. Tabloids are rarely flattering. People love to hate celebrities. Fame is a really difficult business to be in! You are faced with constant criticism and people trying to bring you down every turn. You have to be super confident in who you are to make it in entertainment.

There's too much competition.

Too much rejection.

No one wants to hang out with the insecure woman or guy who looks like they're going to fall to pieces every five seconds. Needy, insecure people are the most draining people you could ever be around. Insecurity breeds insecurity. Avoid these people at all costs! You want to hang out with the person who is doing their thing and having a great time and don't give a shit what everyone around thinks of them. You want to hang out with those people! You want to have sex with those people! You want to *be* those people!

*

Confidence is attractive and, just like a magnet, it attracts!

I'm not talking about cockiness or arrogance. Arrogance is still insecurity. Some guy who's arrogant is defensive and hostile. I'm mild mannered. I'm a nice guy. You don't have to agree with me or like me for me to be confident about who I am and what I believe in.

What you think of me will never change what I think of myself.

The same is true for you: what others think of you, will never change what you see looking back at you in the mirror each day.

The biggest mistake people make is trying to change who they really are to be part of a group. Reverse that. Make yourself the magnet. When you discover who you are and are confident in just being yourself, you will attract people who want to be around you. It's a fact.

You become the confident magnet.

Even in 9th grade, everywhere I went I'd hear people say, "Who's that guy?" They'd point at me, "Who is that kid?" I was put on this pedestal right then and there. The confidence you get from that, along with my look and getting the respect from the masses was everything. It included my elders, my teachers, my family, my neighbors, everybody! My parents were like, "Wow! Where did this kid come from?"

I was the King of Confidence. I knew then, at a very young age, confidence goes a very long way. If you have that, the doors just open up. You get noticed without even trying! When you walk into a room with confidence, people notice. Everyone looks at you and thinks, "Who is that person?" You walk into a room with insecurities? Nobody looks at you. If you're pretending to be something you're not just to try and fit in. Forget it, people see right through you. You know they do! You can tell if someone's a phony, can't you?

I was, and still am, a rocker. I knew it in my gut. I knew rock n' roll music was a part of my soul, even back when I was 15. I'm over 40 now. You have to remember the time. Rock n' roll was in my soul back in the early '80's. This was before any hair bands were around yet. Motley Crue. Poison. They didn't' exist yet. So my look, my persona, hadn't caught on. I didn't even try to look the way I did. I just went with what my hair naturally did and dressed the way I wanted to dress. Nobody else dressed like me. I even made and dyed my own clothes because I couldn't buy the stuff I wanted to wear.

The thing is, even though I wasn't copying anybody in existence, I was being me. You will never be who you are if you just copy someone else. Everybody has themselves. You are yourself – to a point. But that's where it has to start. Once you are confident with who you are and become yourself, that's the most confidence you will ever have. Nobody can ever take that away from you.

You will be influenced by your parents, teachers, neighbors, friends, enemies. Only let those influences build up your confidence. Never let the negative influences tear you down, no matter what. Only pay attention to those words and actions that reflect who you know you really are.

I was a rocker. If my parents had insisted on me being a football player in high school, it wouldn't have worked. I would have failed. They would have failed. Parents need to encourage and support who their kids really are instead of trying to make their kids into something the parents wish they were.

If you're copying people or trying to be something you're really not, you'll never be confident. You won't be yourself! You're a fraud! Until you are you, you can never pull it off. And that is the most empowering trait you could ever have in your life.

In every chapter of this book, it all starts with confidence. If you are not willing to be yourself and you're just looking to do what someone else is doing, or if you're just lazy and want someone else to tell you what to do, then you should stop reading this book right now.

Nothing else in the book will make a difference unless you start with the confidence to just be yourself.

Your true self.

Your honest self.

You have to like yourself first. People who are frauds, who are insecure, who try to be something they're not or try to just copy others are not only miserable in their own skin, they are miserable to be around.

Do you think someone like that can be successful?

No! They don't have an ounce of confidence in their soul.

When people don't like themselves, when they have no confidence, they try to make everyone else around them feel bad so they can feel better in comparison. These people need to be left alone – completely alone! Don't waste any energy on them. Never waste your time on people who are mean to you. That level of insecurity is like the plague. It helps no one and only inflicts misery.

Divorce him or her.

Quit the job.

De-friend whoever is treating you bad in every interaction.

If you're trying to build up your own confidence, you can't have these kinds of people in your life.

*

Do you know why most people fail?

They are afraid of change.

If you don't like who you are right now and if you don't have confidence, then you have to change it. If you're afraid of change, you are going to keep doing the same shit day after day and nothing will improve. You can't keep doing the same things over and over again and wonder why you getting the same results.

"I eat McDonald's Big Macs everyday and I'm still fat!"

Really?

You need someone to point out this out to you?

If you don't like your body, change it. Go on a diet or work out or whatever.

Don't like your hair or the way you dress? Change it up!

Don't like your friends? Hang out with different people!

Don't like the crowds where you hang out? Go somewhere else!

If you don't know yourself well enough to be confident about who you are, then you have to change it up until you find those things that fit and feel right to you.

You have to be honest with yourself, first. Really honest. If you can't do that, then you won't make it. You can't be 80 pounds and look in the mirror and think you're fat. That's not honesty. People lie to themselves more than they lie to others and sometimes those lies can be self destructive.

Most people are afraid of change. Personally, I don't understand that. I love change! I hate being bored. If I'm bored at a place, I'll leave and go somewhere else. If I'm bored at a party, I'll just leave. If I'm bored with the person I'm talking to, I'll end the conversation immediately and talk to someone else.

If you're afraid of change, then take little steps.

The key, though, is to just change something. Change your morning routine. Re-arrange your furniture. Change your hair color. Go to a different bar after work. Cancel your cable TV and meet one of your neighbors. Sell your TV and buy a guitar.

TV is by far the biggest waste of time and the biggest drain on human existence that ever was. If you don't have TV in your house, you'll be forced to do something else.

I dare you to try it.

You also have to get comfortable with failure. You are going to fuck up and fall down. It's part of being human. How are you going to know what you're good at and what you suck at if you don't try different shit! Not everybody wakes up and knows for a fact they're great at playing rock music. I know that. Not everyone is me. But I was never afraid to keep trying other stuff and if I failed, I'd try something else or I'd do the same thing in a different way.

You have to fuck up in order to get confident. You need something to compare it to. How will you ever know you succeeded at something if you didn't fuck it up first?

*

After I became me in 9th grade and was confident, I used to cut school every day and hitchhike to Kern studios. One day my principal followed me.

"Where are you going?" he asked.

"I'm going to the studio to record." It was a simple response. It was what I wanted to do and he wasn't going to stop me.

The principle walked into the studio with me and began talking with the owner.

"You can't let this kid be here. He's supposed to be in school. He's underage," he said.

I'll never forget this conversation as long as I live as it changed my life. The owner knew me. He knew I had the confidence to succeed in music and he wasn't going to let the principle take me away.

"Look, this kid has a lot of talent. You need to let him come here."

And do you know what? The principal just left me there. He didn't drag me back to school!

A couple weeks later, I was called to the principal's office. "Look, we want to make you a deal. We haven't talked to your parents yet, but we talked to the studio owner and he's willing to let you work there and record for free."

I was thrilled.

I was the first kid ever in the state of Delaware to do the work study program. They made it just for me, because they actually believed in me.

They believed in me because I believed in myself first.

I wasn't cut out for school. I knew that. I'm not an academic.

Look at me on the cover of this book. Do I look like I read? My teachers knew I wasn't cut out for school. My parents knew I wasn't college material. I've been educated by the people of the streets from all walks of life all over the world. That's more than any history book I'll never read. Just because I'm not educated in the traditional sense doesn't mean I haven't learned. In fact, I think I'm smarter than many college educated people I've met over the years! I've had people with Ph.D's ask for my advice!

You have to keep trying different things. If you really like music, do you notice if you have a good rhythm? Maybe you should try drums. Or maybe you're a great dancer. Go to the clubs and dance. Introduce yourself to musicians and hang out with them. Check out if you enjoy the same music and see if they'll teach you something. If not, keep moving on. Keep moving until you find that one thing that makes you confident.

Never tell others what you're doing - just do it.

Let those around you see the transformation in you for themselves. When you start trying new things, going to different places, testing out new skills, and having new experiences, people will notice. Trust me, they will.

If they ask you what you've done or what you are doing to change, don't give an answer. Just say, "I'm just trying new stuff." Let people notice the change developing in you and watch how differently they treat you.

Find the confidence that makes you a rock star in your life.

CHAPTER 3

THE POWER OF DIFFERENCE

Your only value in life is how you differ from everyone else.

You have the confidence.

Now you need to stand out from the crowd.

You need to show the world how different you are and how you're unique. If you just blend in with the world around you, no one will notice you and you won't get support for your dream. If you are just like everyone else, why would anyone notice you?

They won't.

If you look at a carton of eggs, does any one egg stand out from the rest? No! Now take one out, replace it with a brown one, and look at the carton of eggs again.

What do you see?

Eleven white eggs?

No! You see the single brown egg in a sea of white.

It's true. Try it.

Make yourself unique. Be the brown egg in a carton of white ones.

*

My girlfriend and I went to a live taping of the "Prairie Home Companion" radio show. Halfway through the show, the host Garrison Keillor, always reads a select few messages on air that have been written by audience members. The messages are dropped into a basket during the show then given to Mr. Keillor. On the day we went, there were a least five hundred messages in the basket by the time it got to us. Without some sort of difference, the chance of our message being chosen and read, was very slim.

Virtually impossible.

I had to figure out a way for our message to stand out from all of the others. I had to make my message the brown egg in the sea of white ones.

So just as the basket when up to the host, I took our piece of paper, our message, folded it into a paper airplane, and stuck it in the corner of the basket. Do you know what happened?

It was the first one they picked.

Our message was picked out of hundreds of others and read live to all of the show's listeners around the world!

I call this The Power of Difference.

*

What does that special message in the basket teach you? It teaches you that being unique makes a difference. Difference gets noticed. I hang out at bars during happy hour surrounded by men in business suits and ties. They all look the same. They all shop at the same store and get the same hair cut. You might think I look ridiculous sitting around all these business people with my black clothes, black hair, and black hat. I don't care. I look different and I stand out therefore, I look like the more interesting person to talk to in the room.

Not fitting in isn't always bad. This was a contest to get people to come to downtown Minneapolis, find me, and take a picture. I was so different in Minneapolis that I was easy to recognize.

*

Think about it. If you had a choice of talking to a guy in a suit, talking to another faceless drone on his Smartphone, while typing an email on his laptop or someone else, someone who is uniquely different, who will you choose?

You will choose the guy who stands out.

Why?

Because, if you're smart, you'll see that person and think, "I bet I can learn something from that guy."

Fifteen minutes of fame is easy to come by - your difference gets your foot in the door. Your confidence seals the deal and turns the fifteen minutes into a lifetime. Without the confidence, your fifteen minutes becomes two. Everything, including the Power of Difference, connects to the Power of Confidence.

Talk about looking different! Looking different only gets you noticed. It's up to you after that.

I wasn't LA Nik in L.A. I didn't become LA Nik until I moved to Minneapolis.

People would walk up to me and say, "Who are you?"

"I'm Nik," I'd tell them.

"Where do you live?"

"L.A."

So everyone started calling me LA Nik. I'm not even from L.A. I'm *from* Philly! I *lived* in L.A.

Now, though, Minneapolis is my home.

Throughout my life, I've lived in many cities up and down both coasts. This is the only place I've lived where there were no other rockers like me. In Minneapolis, I'm the only "Hollywood Rocker" around.

Staff photos by Bob Herbert

"Niki" (left), who was visiting from Los Angeles, chats with his friend Johnie Bates at the Metal Shop.

I'm unique.

I'm different.

I'm the brown egg in the sea of white ones. I'm the guy with the black fedora in a sea of business suits, briefcases, and Smartphones.

Within weeks of living here in Minneapolis, I'd received a double-page spread in a local magazine. I'd been interviewed on radio and television. I couldn't stop the promotion I was receiving. Why? Because I was different from anyone else in the city. They had never encountered someone as different as me.

People are very cautious here in the Midwest. But they accepted me. I'm confident in my difference. That was key. You can be different all you want, but if you don't have an ounce of confidence, you become a joke. In Los Angeles, I see people lock their car doors at street corners when they see me.

Not here.

Here in Minneapolis, people shake my hand and say "Hi."

I'm different. They want to learn from me.

*

If you take a letter to the photocopier, make a copy, make a copy of the copy, make a copy of the copy of the copy, it eventually becomes unreadable. Eventually, the copy becomes just a mass of black ink. That's what happens to you when you try to be just like everyone else – you become indistinguishable from everyone else.

You stop growing.

You stop progressing in life.

What would happen if a company started to hire the same people with the same skill set? They would eventually become stagnant. Their products will become uninteresting and dull. They will not be able to compete with other companies who are hiring talent with the latest and greatest knowledge.

In months, they'd probably declare bankruptcy and close their doors.

Does this sound familiar?

Think about corporate life where things have become dull and stagnant. They've become "corporatized." Everyone is in the same suit and tie. Black shoes. White shirt. Same haircut. Same tie. People have become drones. No one sticks out. Everyone is afraid to be unique – to be different. The same happens to their products.

What about the companies who are energized by change – by difference. Who embrace it. People stand in lines to buy their products – and pay lots of money for them.

When you have to apply for a job and turn in a resume, how are you going to make your resume stand out among five hundred other candidates? If you apply to a company that doesn't like difference, they'll probably frown on a "different" resume. It doesn't fit their corporate standard. It will end up in the trash can.

Why would you want to work there?

Personally, if I was actually applying for a job, I'd do my resume on black paper with white ink. It would stand out in a stack of white paper and get noticed! Companies who relish difference would embrace my resume and pick it from the basket in the sea of white ones.

If you have confidence in who you are, you will always be different and you will stand out. Your difference becomes part of you – it becomes a natural extension of *you.* If you don't have confidence and you just try to blend in, you will just follow the herd and you'll be a photocopied version of yourself – you'll become indistinguishable from everyone else.

Don't photocopy your life. Embrace your difference and show it in its true form.

*

The easiest way to stand out is in the way you look. When I was in high school back in Delaware, I was the only one who looked like I did. I was doing the rocker look long before it became popular. Remember, there was no Internet and the top metal bands weren't known yet. But I knew who I was *inside* and I wanted to show who I was on the *outside.*

When you are confident in who you are on the inside you should show it in the way you look! Just because you might have a job that requires you to wear a uniform or a suit doesn't mean you have to wear a "home suit" of khakis or sweatpants when you're not at work. You're free to be yourself. Experiment with the way you look. Find what works and makes you stand out in the crowd.

Confidence will always stand out. But you also want to look like someone interesting to talk to.

When I went to L.A., I looked like a lot of rockers in the area. But the one thing that made me stand out was I shaved my head on one side. No one else did that then! Other guys ended up copying me!

If you dress like everyone else, use the same words, communicate the same as everyone else, watch the same TV shows, have the same hobbies, and listen to the same music as everyone else, where's your value? How are you different?

You're not.

The fact is, everyone is different!

You have to find yours.

You have to play around with the way you look and you have to try different things to find out what makes you, *you.* Instead of finding a group and trying to fit in, you should find out who you are first and then find the people you fit with. People do it backwards all the time.

How you look is like advertisement. When you go out in public, how you look can attract people you'd want to meet. This is why a lot of artistic or gothic kids look like they do. They want to hang around others like them. I was already dressing like a rocker and I wanted to hang with other rockers. Music can be the great congregator. It's the easiest thing to have in common with someone and can be the starting point for great friendships.

Advertise yourself!

Promote yourself!

Show who you are on the inside by the way you look on the outside. People will find you interesting and will want to talk to you. Don't be afraid to stand out. If you're already confident in who you are, who you really are, you will want the attention!

*

If you are not different, it is virtually impossible to progress in life. In order to learn, to create, and to share you have to have a difference in life.

If you hang out with the same group of people day in and day out and they are duplicates of yourself (because you don't have the confidence to branch out), then there is absolutely no way for you to progress. There will be nothing for you to learn – because everyone knows the same thing. There will be nothing to create – because it will have been done already. There will be nothing for you to share – because no one will be interested in what you have to say!

It's true!

If you always go to the same old bar with the same group of friends, and cheer for the same sports team, change it up! Go to the bar where the opposing team's fans go and wear the cap from your team (the opposing team). You will be different! You will be noticed.

You will learn from them.

You will create new opportunities for yourself.

You will be able to share what you have learned with others.

Wherever you're going, find out how you can stand out in that crowd. I go to a bar that's filled with suit-wearing investment bankers. I wear a black fedora, eyeliner, black pants, a black leather jacket, and black nail polish.

Do you think I'm different in this bar?

Fuck yes!

I stand out!

And the business men and women want to talk to me because obviously, someone with my confidence is brave enough to stand out in that crowd and not be intimidated.

*

You have to be willing to change. I woke up in 9th grade and knew who I was but I continued to grow – to continue to grow and learn. You have to exercise your brain each and every day and constantly change.

Everyone is afraid to change, but change is good! I say this a lot, and I mean it! Changing to stand out in whatever crowd you happen to be in is the Power of Difference. If you do the same thing every day, look the same way every day, go to the same places, the same stores, buy the same food, see the same people and remain in a routine day in and day out, you will slowly lose the stimulation you need to evolve and you will lose your confidence, lose your dream, and you'll never stand out and make a difference.

Basically, you have a choice: you can live off other people's lives or you can make your own.

Never remain stagnant.

Being in a rut and continuing to live in the past won't get you anywhere towards the future. Pay attention to your environment and what's around you – learn, create, and share. Then find a way to be different and stand out in that environment.

CHAPTER 4

POWER OF PLACE

Don't just maintain your life. Live your life.

The Power of Place is essential for the evolution of *you*. Along with Confidence and Difference, it's another vital building block in your growth. I learned very early on that if I wanted to be noticed, I had to diversify – to expand beyond my home, my hometown, even beyond my family and friends. I had to get out of the comfort zone that I had grown up in and jump off the cliff I'd grown accustomed to my entire life. I wanted to be a rocker but being a rocker in Delaware didn't make sense. It just wasn't going to happen! So I moved. I used the Power of Place to launch my career and progress in my life.

- If all you ever do is stay home and watch TV, you will never progress in life.
- If the only people you hang out with are people you work with, you will never progress in life.
- If the only people you do activities with are your family, you will never progress in life.
- If you never live anywhere outside of the area you were born, you will never progress in life.

The Power of Place.
Go where you don't belong.
Evolve.

Helping a sick friend haul grain in North Dakota. I learned a lot about a different way of life and people different from myself.

*

If you want to be noticed – if you want to really, truly progress in your life, how can you do that if you hang around with people and in places that are clones of yourself?

The reality of it is that you won't. You're stuck.

I don't watch a lot of television, but I've heard about some of the winners on *American Idol*. The market for that television show is primarily for the "under 25" group. That market is supposed to listen to hip hop and pop - maybe a little rock. Even less country. But who has been their most successful winners? The kids who have entered the contest and sang country songs! Carrie Underwood is a perfect example.

She went where she probably didn't really belong and stood out from all of the others. She was noticed. She was able to display her talent to a group of people who would not of otherwise heard of her. Now look at her.

She's a huge star!

Carrie Underwood probably tried the traditional route that all country singers travel. They sing at home – everyone probably told her that she was incredible. Everyone told her that she had talent and needed to be a country star. She was probably told to "go to Nashville!" I have no idea if she did, but if so, she evidently failed because she wasn't a star when she tried out for American Idol. Why would she fail in Nashville? Because everyone in Nashville sings country music! She was selling the same product as everyone else there! If she did go to Nashville, she was definitely exercising The Power of Place. But on the other hand, there was no Power of Difference.

The Power of Difference and the Power of Place go hand in hand.

Finding myself in the middle of nowhere - and I mean finding myself.

You can move from one place to another, but if you take the easy route and go to someplace familiar, where everyone is still like you, you will still not progress. Go someplace where you are unique. Go to where your qualities will outshine everyone else – and you will succeed.

*

I've used the Power of Place to my advantage throughout my life. I like to visit different bars. Bars where I am clearly different. Look at the cover of this book again. Do I look someone who'd belong in a cowboy bar?

No.

But I go to them.

I go to cowboy bars just like I also visit biker bars and "business" bars (bars with investment bankers in suits). When I walk into a biker bar, I seem to fit in. People see me walk in then immediately ignore me. In business bars and cowboy bars, I'm different. People notice me and start talking to me. Asking me what I'd be doing in "this" bar?

It's great! I learn so much from being in different places. I'm able to create new friends and share my experiences with them. A great example of this was when I was twenty years old and still living in Delaware.

I was sitting in a bar called Cowboys at two o'clock in the afternoon. There was no one in the bar except this old man and me - he looked just as out of place as I did. He didn't look like a cowboy. He wasn't wearing a hat. He didn't have cowboy boots on. As a matter of fact, he almost looked down on his luck – kinda dirty. I learned that his name was Mr. Weihe. We struck up a conversation and he told me that he was from Virginia but he owned a house in Delaware called Baynard Hall.

I knew this house!

Everybody knew this house. It was the biggest, oldest historical house in the area. There was a plaque outside and a museum. It was the only place in Delaware where a civil war battle was fought. By chance, I meet the guy who owns it.

It was the Power of Place in action.

I really wanted to see the house. So I started asking more questions about the mansion.

"I bet it's a really cool place."

"Do you want to see it?" he asked.

"Absolutely!"

The opportunity was perfect and the mansion was everything that I'd expected.

The mansion had twenty-foot ceilings, a huge grand piano, and enormous curtains from floor to ceiling. Everything is in its original 1830's style. There was massive art everywhere. All the furniture was original from 1832.

This was my home when I was 21 - Baynard Hall

As he is showing me around the place, he suddenly says, "How would you like to live here?"

"Are you serious?" I was dumbfounded. I thought he was joking.

"I'm looking for someone to live here and take care of the place."

How could I say no?

So the next day, he hands me the keys and he goes back to Virginia.

Here I am, twenty years old, in a ten-bedroom house, fully furnished from 1832, with a guest house next door, and a two-car garage outside.

Next thing I know, I have 2 bands living there – Psychopath and my band, The Unexpected. Everybody just moved in. I lived here for 2 years and it was a party each and every day.

There wasn't a single closet in the house - just big armoires. There was no wiring in the original house so when it was eventually wired, all the light switches were way up high.

The house had massive, twenty foot long paintings. There was one on a hallway wall that was a painting of the Roman Empire after it fell. It was an absolutely beautiful work of art.

It was a pretty cool experience for me. It was the Power of Place. You never know who you're going to meet unless you get out and try different places. The vast majority of people I've met who have helped me in some way and have become long term, close friends of mine were people I met by chance in some random place.

Another party at Baynard Hall.

*

You are never going to know who you'll meet in this life if you don't get out there. This is true for establishing friendships, finding a mate, making business connections, trying out new experiences. Who are you going to meet sitting at home? How many different experiences can you have on the couch?

As with building up your confidence, going after a dream, standing out in a crowd – you have to change things up! I went to a lot of different clubs and I frequented my favorites. But I didn't have a regular routine. Sometimes I'd be at a club every night of the week for a month. Then I wouldn't go back for two months because I was trying different places.

And whenever I went back, people were always excited to see me again. I was unpredictable with my routines and when you're unpredictable about where you go, you create a certain mystery about you. People never knew if I was going to show up to a party or not. When I did, I was always welcomed with enthusiasm.

People have said I'm a hard person to get to know. I don't understand that. I'm an open book! What you see is what you get. But when you're unpredictable in your routine, you create some mystery and it keeps people interested in you because they'll never know where you're going to show up next, how long you'll stay or who you'll bring along.

Remember Norm from that show "Cheers"? He sat in the same spot at the bar, and ordered the same beer at the same time every day. I know he was a fictional character, but these guys exist at every bar. They don't do anything other than take up space. They become an invisible piece of the bar's décor. You get used to them being there and then they are not noticed. They just let life happen around them instead of being an active part of life.

What's the point in going out if you're just going to sit back and watch other people live? You might as well go home and watch TV. It's the same thing. You have to interact with your environment. You have to talk to people.

You will not find your soul mate if you only go to the same bar after work every night hoping things will change. Hope only gets you so far. Time to go somewhere else and try something new! I hear people whine about this all the time! They want to meet someone to share their life with but they keep going to the same hang out they always go to and they wonder why they never meet anyone. Well, if you've been going there for that long, you've become part of the décor – just like Norm - and no one notices you're there. They may know your name, but that's about it.

Go to a new place where you stand out and get noticed. If you're in a business suit, go to a coffee shop. It doesn't mean you'll find your soul mate, but you never know! At least you'll stand out and if your soul mate is there, he or she will notice you.

People don't like to step out of their comfort zone – people are essentially afraid of change. People like familiarity. It makes people feel safe. But if you don't get out of your comfort zone once in awhile, you'll never be anything more than you are right now.

If you grew up in Pittsburgh, your parents are from Pittsburgh, your friends are from Pittsburgh, and all your friends and family work in construction, then you'll be expected to work in construction and live in Pittsburgh for the rest of your life.

And, more than likely, you will do exactly that.

But what if your dream was to own your own business? What if you were really passionate about software design, for example, and were confident about your ability to work in technology? If the thing you want to do isn't going to happen where you live, MOVE!

I was never going to be a rock star in Delaware. Can you name the last great rock band to come out of Delaware?

No?

I rest my case.

*

The Power of Place is intoxicating. Some may call it being at the right place at the right time. If you're always in the same place though, the odds of something good happening are slim.

Diversify.

Spread out.

What if you'd been in the right place to by Apple® stock when it was $1.00 a share? What about Microsoft® stock?

What if you'd owned or inherited land in western North Dakota? North Dakota is now second only to Texas in oil production.

North Dakota!

A while ago, I read an article in the *USA Today*. It told about the oil boom in North Dakota. Ten years ago, North Dakota was 38th in the country when it came to personal income. Now it's 17th! It has a $1 billion state surplus.

What other state can boast of that?

So. What are you going to do if you lose your job?

Are you going to stick around and wait for someone to come to you and offer you a job? Wait for things to turn around? Collect unemployment? Fuck no!

Move!

North Dakota's unemployment is barely above 5%. In Detroit its 18%. In Las Vegas it's almost 12%.

Move!

Use the Power of Place to your advantage. If you just wait around for opportunity to come to you, you will fail. It's pure and simple. Don't wait.

Move!

If you don't move to where opportunity can present itself, you become stagnant. You stop learning, creating, and sharing. The minute you move to someplace new, you start the engines going again. You start to learn. Once you learn you start to create again.

Now you're on a roll.

Now you can begin sharing.

*

I'm not a religious person, but the Power of Place even goes back to biblical times.

So it's definitely nothing new.

Have you ever heard the story of Joseph?

Joseph was sold into slavery by his brothers and taken to Egypt. A Hebrew in Egypt – he definitely had the Power of Difference to his advantage. Now he had to use the Power of Place.

He monopolized his knowledge and his skills as a herder and farmer to learn the Egyptian culture. He created a proposal to store the Pharaoh's grain for times of famine and drought. When he shared it with Pharaoh, the leader was so pleased that he made Joseph his Vizier (his chief advisor).

You have to move to where your dream can be fulfilled – to live your life. Sometimes you are not given a choice about the place – sometimes events dictate actions. However, this bible story tells us that everybody has a place where they can do better than where they are.

*

Most people are not born in the right place for them to be successful. Look, maybe it was the right place for you to grow up as a kid, but when you get to be an adult, you're not that kid anymore and you can go where ever you want. Staying in your home town and not venturing out to find something else will start you on that path to stagnation.

You'll be tolerated, not celebrated, in your home town. They already know you. You need to go where you can be celebrated and you need to surround yourself with people who celebrate and appreciate who you are. The people you grew up with? They'll never see you as anything more than what you used to be.

Never get too comfortable fitting in. You'll never be different if you just fit in to the crowd. Always move around and be the center of attention. Once you start to get comfortable where you are, move.

I'm serious.

Your brain wants to continue to evolve and grow. When you live too long in comfort, your brain doesn't learn anything new, it just maintains.

If you check out a new place and you feel uncomfortable, good! Stay and talk to people until you do feel comfortable. Most people would immediately pack up and head home to live in their parent's basement. We're all just people. You're not going to be able to talk to everyone in a room if you can't get comfortable talking to one stranger in a bar. You have to practice. You have to start somewhere.

Life isn't meant to be maintained! It's meant to be lived. You're meant to have experiences. You're meant to push the boundaries of comfort.

Learn to live the Power of Place.

CHAPTER 5

THE POWER OF FINESSE

It's not what you say, it's how you say it.

If the Power of Place is an essential building block for the evolution of "you," then The Power of Finesse is an essential building block for the evolution of your relationships and daily life. Finesse is key for every relationship – your mate, your boss, your co-workers.

Everyone.

In order to be a dancer, you have to have finesse. You have to know how to move across the floor. Your mind has to know where to put your foot before you even think about moving it. Comedians have finesse. They can plant a seed with a small one-liner, let it grow, and bring down the house an hour later. The Power of Finesse is all of this and more.

The Power of Finesse is knowing how to say and do the right things at the right time in the right place. It's being charming without being arrogant.

Without finesse, you won't be able to successfully navigate the mine fields of life. The Power of Finesse provides the map to the mine field and helps you steer clear of trouble – the big explosions that can make you detour to places you don't want to venture.

Finesse helps you steer your course – it doesn't help you manipulate it.

*

People are a lot like dogs.

If you chase after a dog, it runs away from you. Right? If you run away from a dog, what does it do? It chases you! People are the same. If you chase people down, they'll run away from you. Wondering what they want and why they want it from you. If you run away from people, they chase you.

This only works if you have confidence though. If you're just some guy walking into a meeting with his head hung down and not making eye contact with anyone, no one is going to notice. No one will even think about chasing him. However, walk into a room with finesse and confidence, your head held high, making eye contact with everyone, what happens?

It's not what you say, it's how you say it. This is me cracking up funny man Alan Kalter; Announcer for the David Letterman show.

They think, "Who the fuck is that? I have to meet this guy."

They become the dogs chasing you!

It's true. It works.

Believe me.

*

Put simply, The Power of Finesse is basically micromanaging your life. Like a dancer who knows where to plant her foot before she even moves it, Finesse is knowing what you are going to say before you say it.

I learned this firsthand about finesse when I owned my automotive restoration business in Florida called Del Rey Vintage. One of my employees taught me a lesson in finesse that I will never forget. He didn't do it intentionally – he was very subtle. As a matter of fact, Rueben probably didn't even know what he was doing, but I remember it like it was yesterday.

He was working on a car of one of my best clients. The problem was that he wasn't doing things correctly – or at least he wasn't in my opinion.

"Rueben. You're fucking this up! You'd better fix that," I yelled.

Do you see what I did wrong?

I didn't at first. It took a couple of subtle lessons from Reuben to set me straight.

Reuben wouldn't say a word. He was too proud. I pushed him out of the way and finished the job myself. The next day, Reuben didn't show up for work. After about four days, he came back, and started work again. He'd be quiet for a while but would eventually be back to normal. It was after this happened a couple of times that I recognized the pattern.

I had about as much finesse as a fat chick in a ballet.

I didn't think about what I said before I said it. I'd lost the map to my life's mine field. Most of all though, I used the word "you" instead of "we." Rueben was a proud man and didn't need to be treated the way I treated him.

By saying "You fucked this up" instead of "I think we're doing this wrong and we should fix it this way," I stepped on a landmine. A fucking big one. I put my employee on the defensive before he even had a chance to respond – before he had the chance to explain or even defend himself.

*

You have to know your limits and how to get things done. You can use business strategies in everyday life and many of life's lessons in business. You have to be careful about being persistent with people because the moment you push, they're going to think you want something from them. As soon as somebody thinks you want something from them, it's over.

You're shut out.

You have to get people to believe you have something to offer.

*

Use the same rules and guidelines for finding your mate and dating as you do in the business world. Remember these four important words: make her chase *you*!

The best solution is to show interest in her without her believing you want something in return. Say you're on your way to work and you walk the same way to the office every day. You're on the same sidewalks day after day. You ride the same elevator. Over time, you will begin to notice the same people – they are just like you after all. Then, one day, you finally get the courage to acknowledge the one person who had piqued your interest after all of this time. You think to yourself, I'd really like to meet her, but you've never said anything to her before. Most people are afraid and self conscious. They would never have the confidence or finesse to approach someone.

Then one day you make a passing compliment. You say, "Cool shoes!"

You don't wait for a reply.

You don't wait for her to say, "Thanks."

You don't wait for a compliment in return.

You just keep on walking.

Do you know what you've done?

You've now made the person curious and she will now notice you the next time.

If you expect and wait for a reply, you'll get shot down. By continuing on your way, she will think, "Wow, he just complimented me for no reason. He must have genuinely meant it." 9 times out of 10 the person will start a conversation the next time you pass one another.

It works.

If people don't think you want something from them, they want to know you. Everybody wants to find a mate. Everybody wants friends. Everybody needs connections in business, in school, whatever.

It's human nature.

*

The Power of Finesse can also be considered common sense.

If you can't deal with a relationship with one person how are you going to deal with any dream you have?

You're not!

Never burn a bridge – ever.

I have no problem telling someone I think they're fucking up. I've just learned how to say it with finesse. I'll tell the truth as I see it – but with style.

I own what I say and take responsibility for my words.

I'll say, "Hey, this is my opinion. But I think you're doing something wrong." I never tell someone I think they're an idiot or stupid. Name calling is immature and it doesn't ever help any situation.

You have to say the right thing to people. Saying the words "we" instead of "you," for example. It is a bit of a game of manipulation, but you will ultimately get what you want and you'll get the other person on board with you. And most importantly, you won't hurt their feelings.

But that's how life is.

Life is a big fucking game and you have to know how to play by its rules. There are all of these things in life they don't teach you in school. Important things like:

There's a difference between being confident and being arrogant.

There's a difference between being persistent and being a stalker.

There's a difference between believing in yourself and being narcissistic.

If you're not sure how to play the game, watch other people who do it with ease.

Learn from those with finesse.

It's why I'm writing this book! I've learned a lot of things in my life and all I want to do is share what I've learned. I've talked to thousands of people and I can't tell you how many people I've helped one-on-one. This book is just about spreading my wisdom to the masses.

Surround yourself around people who seem to know how to play the game. Listen to them. Watch them. Then try it out on other people. Never try to play the game with the professionals. Learn from those you admire and try out their techniques with your own style. You can't quote them. You can't do things exactly the way they do it. You're you and they are who they are. All of these techniques you can use in your personal and professional life.

If your life's foundation is strong, built on integrity, nobody can take you down. Be true to yourself and everyone around you. Do what you say and say what you do. If I tell someone I'll be there, I'll be there. You have to do the same. Be honest with people. Be honest to yourself.

My impression is that most people are not happy with their own lives. I hear this everywhere I go. If it isn't true, then there are a lot of people bitching and complaining for no reason!

What people don't get is that they are in complete control – they've just lost control over time. Everyone has the map to the landmines in their lives. Most just don't know to read the map or even where to find it! They chase the wrong dreams – status and money. Those things don't make you happy.

You have to be happy with yourself.

Dealing with people is just like playing poker. You have to know how to read them just like you have to know what poker hand is the best and what the odds are of completing that inside straight. You have to read the subtle gestures and the small movements. You have to know when you have the upper hand and when you might have to duck from a flying fist.

You have to know when you can call someone's bluff. No one tries to bluff me – I play the game too well. I also don't look like a victim so they don't even try. Most people are intimidated and won't talk to me. The people who do talk to me have the confidence to match mine.

How I look doesn't match my personality. I know that. I look intimidating. I look hard core. Some people may even think I look like a drug addict.

But I know I'm not.

I'm a nice guy. I'm loyal to my mate. I'm a good friend. I keep my promises and I don't hurt people's feelings. But people wouldn't know that about me from looking at me. And I'm fine with that. I'm not interested in knowing those people anyway. I have no tolerance for people who judge before they even have the confidence to approach me and say “hello.” I'm confident about who I am. I know myself. My mate knows me and my friends know me. I don't have to prove anything to everyone in the world.

I get approached mostly by business men. I don't know why. Maybe because they want to be me. Or maybe they wanted to be me when they were younger but then lost it when they entered the rat race. I don’t know.

Maybe they talk to me because I don't have a lot of patience for politeness and small talk and that’s what they’re used to dealing with day in and day out. It's all a mask and it keeps us from being who we really are. I have no filter and I'll say how it is and what I think. I personally believe the world would be a lot better off if people just cut through that bullshit and were just honest with each other.

The world will treat you according to what you think of yourself. I absolutely believe that. I’m real. I’m honest. I’m a good guy and I care.

*

Having finesse is successfully steering your life. You have a choice as to what you want your life to be like.

Do you want it to be a huge ship that takes forever to turn?

Do you want it to be a racecar that if the steering wheel is turned even the slightest, you crash into the side wall.

One is slow and deliberate.

The other is fast and precarious.

You don't want to be the Titanic but you also don't want to be crashing at every turn. Life is a compromise between the two. You must have the finesse to make quick decisions like the race car but the patience to let things take their course – like the cruise ship.

Humans are not naturally born with finesse.

Finesse is acquired. It is learned from practice – from time on life's stage.

The problem that I have witnessed is that most people become the cruise ship. They become so mired in living the dream that they cannot make the fast decisions that they once could. A few years ago I met a man at a bar and started up a conversation. He was dressed in a suit and tie. He had a cell phone, a laptop, and an earpiece so he could talk on the phone without lifting his hand. He told me that he worked for a large company. He was one of the ninety presidents of the ninety divisions within the company.

He had pretty business cards.

"How the fuck do you get anything done?" I asked.

He laughed and said, "We don't. It takes way too long. When we were smaller, things were different though. It was a lot more fun back then. We're a global company now and that's pretty cool though. I get to travel now."

The guy was miserable. I could read it on his face, hear it in his voice, and see it in his eyes.

True. He made a lot of money but he was lost in the machine. He was on his third wife and his kids didn't talk to him. He had once worked for a company that was a combination cruise ship and race car. He now worked on the Titanic. The icebergs were coming and they were too big to steer clear. The company had lost the map to guide them through life.

A year later, I came across his business card.

It was still pretty.

I recognized the company's name from the news. It had just closed its doors and thousands of people had lost their jobs.

*

As I have said, The Power of Finesse is an essential building block for the evolution of your life. Finesse is the art of micromanaging yourself. It's not manipulation. It's not lying.

It's timing.

Timing to know what to say and when to say it.

Timing to know when to turn from an approaching iceberg or landmine and being agile enough to realize that danger is coming.

You will only gain the Power of Finesse from living your life - it's not something that you wake up with. Finesse takes time. You don't want to be a charming Yes-Man - you want to be the one that other people chase. The Power of Finesse is being able to balance the fine line between knowing when to be quiet and when to brag.

CHAPTER 6

THE POWER OF COMMUNICATION

Don't just talk. Communicate.

The Power of Communication, like Finesse, is learned. You are not born with it and, like most lessons in this book, it's acquired through experience.

Are you a teenager? Then you must learn to effectively communicate now – don't wait until it's too late. Impress them in a job interview by being able to not just talk, but communicate.

There is a difference.

Talking and communicating are as different as apples and oranges.

A two year old can talk but not really communicate an idea besides the essentials of life like hunger and thirst.

As you mature, your vocabulary expands but without practice, your ability to communicate becomes stagnant. It's not because of stupidity but because the skill has not been exercised enough. Treat communication like a muscle – the more you try, the better you get, and the stronger the muscle becomes. Maturity brings the life experiences to help build the skills needed to effectively communicate and to make the muscle solid.

Communication is a combination of confidence and finesse and once you have it, the world can be yours.

*

There are certain places that do not have a great reputation when it comes to customer service. We all dread having to go to them but we've all had to go: the Post Office and DMV. Most believe that the people who work there have the worst jobs on the face of the Earth. Maybe they do. That's not what's important though. What's important is that the people who work there deserve the same respect as anyone else. The fact that you hate having to go there is not their fault. When people have to bite the bullet and go, they treat the employees with distain and disrespect.

It's a self-fulfilling prophecy.

The people have a reputation of being rude so customers treat them rude so the employees in turn are rude in return. They are more focused on the end of their shift! It's a no-win situation for anyone.

What if you went in the DMV with a different attitude?

What if you accepted that these people do, indeed, probably have the worst jobs known to man but they have to make a living. They have bills to pay. A family to support. They listen to people complain all day about the bureaucracy but are helpless to do anything about it. Plus, if someone is rude to them, why should they bother being helpful?

I know I wouldn't.

What if you went in with a different attitude?

What if you decide to communicate rather than talk?

I've learned to communicate – not talk – and I use my skills of communication every minute of every day.

It works every time.

When I moved back to Los Angeles, I lost everything. I didn't have a single form of identification on me and without a driver's license,

I couldn't do anything. So I had to make a trip to the DMV. I took my number and watched the people interact. It was not pleasant. As my number was approaching, I started to watch and guess who would be the person to be helping me. I watched as they interacted with the customers and I watched how the customers interacted with them. Every single customer was fucking rude. If I was going to get an ID, I knew I'd have to be different. The person I'd watched the longest turned out call my number.

"Fifty-two," she yelled. That was my number. I could tell that she was having a bad day. After all, the person she'd just tried to help had just called her a fat bitch and walked away in disgust.

"I don't know how you deal with that," I said. "That was uncalled for."

"It's part of the job," she said. I could tell she was just waiting to get to the next customer so she could end her day. I also thought I could see her eyes water. After all, she'd just been called a fat bitch.

"It doesn't make it right. No one deserves to be treated that way." Then I noticed that she was wearing a beautiful necklace. "That is a beautiful necklace," I said. If you remember from the previous chapter, The Power of Finesse, I didn't wait for her to compliment me and I didn't immediately tell her my problem.

"Thank you. My husband gave it to me for our thirtieth anniversary."

She was letting her guard down. She knew I wasn't going to be a threat. She realized that I was a nice guy despite my appearance and that I wasn't going to be another one of her typical customers who just shout and complain. She was so used to being yelled at that it was refreshing to have someone communicate with her instead of threaten and demand.

"How can I help you?"

She was actually smiling and she was actually looking at me instead of at her computer monitor.

"I have lost everything," I said. "My driver's license, my credit cards. I honestly don't know what to do next."

"Well, let's see what I can do," she said.

If I had been just another Californian, I'm sure I would have had to go to another line, fill out forms, wait some more, fill out more forms, wait a week, and maybe then have a driver's license. By using the Power of Communication, I walked out with a new driver's license in about one hour. More importantly, I'd made a new friend. Her name was Martha. Her husband was Ben. She had three kids and four grandchildren.

Communicating with your mate is a delicate balance. Just like with anyone. Try to say, "we" instead of, "you" or "me."

*

Using the Power of Communication is like gardening. It takes patience. When you plant a seed, does it immediately take root and sprout? No. It takes days or even weeks before you know that what you planted is going to take root and grow.

The same is true for the ideas and concepts you communicate in your business and professional life.

If there's a position at work that suddenly becomes open, the best approach is not to immediately run in to your boss' office and demand to be given the promotion and raise. Treat work like your garden.

Plant seeds then wait for them to grow.

One of the most important lessons of communication is to *prove* your point (your value) before your *make* your point. Be positive. Let your boss know that you are valuable. Demonstrate your ability to do the job then plant the seed with, "I could do that."

Then drop the conversation.

You've planted the seed now be patient and let it take hold. The thing to remember is that the squeaky wheel gets the grease. If you squeak too much you get replaced.

*

Like most everything else I've talked about in this book, communication requires confidence. If you don't have confidence when you communicate, then none of your seeds will germinate.

None.

Without confidence, you're talking again – not communicating. Everyone will hear what you are saying but no one will react. To them, you're just another voice among hundreds of others.

You've become noise.

Let's say that you've left your laptop in a hotel conference room. You need your laptop so you walk up to the concierge. Your head is down, you don't make eye contact, and you say, "Pardon me, but if it's not too much trouble and if you have time, can you please let me in the conference room to get my laptop?"

You've placed yourself below the concierge. He's not going to help. Why would he? You've given him lots of opportunity to say no. You've said "if you have time." You've said "if it's not too much trouble."

That's not communication.

That's talking without confidence.

In order to effectively communicate, put yourself at the same level as the person you are talking to. Make eye contact. Keep your head up.

"I need to get into that locked room to get my laptop."

Don't wait for him to reply. Start walking towards the locked room.

Make the concierge chase you!

CHAPTER 7

THE POWER OF RESPONSIBILITY

Life is short. Why make it shorter?

None of us are worth anything without others. We have to respect and care for others in our lives in order to fulfill our own. Everything we do has a consequence that can affect others either in a positive or negative way.

This was a very hard lesson for me to learn.

But I did – it just took a while.

You may not know me, but others can attest to the fact that when I've only had $10 in my pocket,

I've given $5 of it to someone else who needed it more.

It's the Power of Responsibility.

Police officer Pat McCarver (left) wins the "Take a Pic of L.A. Nik" contest and intern gives a portion of his winnings to a family in need.

We are all responsible for our own lives. If on your death bed, you have nothing but regrets, then the only person you have to blame is yourself.

Did you work at the same job for twenty years only to have your salary increase by $3 an hour?

Change it up!

It's your responsibility to change your job or career. It's not your boss' fault. It's not your mate's fault.

It's yours.

Your actions and inactions have consequences. It's up to you to be responsible to understand and deal with them as they happen

*

One of my first lessons about responsibility and consequences happened in 1987. I was taking a break from touring with the band I was in, "Saints in Hell," and had decided to take my girlfriend to the Bahamas. We were staying in Nassau but decided to visit Cat Island. Cat Island is in the central Bahamas and is one of its districts. Mount Alvernia, the highest point in the Bahamas is there and there is actually a monastery at its top. We took a small plane from Nassau to Cat Island. The airport on the island wasn't big. It didn't have gates like you'd expect. We landed on the tarmac and just walked off of the plane. As we walked away from the plane, I noticed a group of three or four guys. They looked at me, waved, and shouted, "MTV! MTV!" They didn't know who I was but assumed from my appearance that I was in the music industry. I was "MTV."

We decided to rent a motorcycle and take in the sites Cat Island had to offer. Part-way though our trip, we stopped at a small bar that looked more like a shack in the middle of nowhere. The same guys that were yelling "MTV!" at the airport were there. As soon as we walked in to the bar, one guy walked up to me and said, "Hey! Wanna do some coke in the bathroom?"

I didn't see the harm so I left my girlfriend by the motorcycle, joined the guys, and did a few lines of coke. All of a sudden the door was kicked in and there were people yelling, shoving others around, and securing everyone with zip ties. Everyone was daisy-chained together like a

Christmas decoration. No one was going anywhere.

I saw the owner of the club and said to him, "Hey, I was just using the bathroom. I just got here." They must have believed me so they let me go. The owner whispered, "Just go. Go far away."

When I went outside to rejoin my girlfriend she said, "Hey the keys to the motorcycle are in the helmet. It's on a table in the bar!" The owner was having none of it. He wanted us out. "Look, come back later. Just get out of here now," he said.

We had no choice so we left and came back four hours later. But things hadn't changed. The next thing I know, my hands were being zip-tied behind my back. They lead me outside to a van and drove me to the island's jail. In order to process me, they asked for my driver's license. Mine was from Delaware and they had no idea what or where Delaware was. It took another half-hour for me to explain that it was in the United States and not too far from New York.

"New York!" they yelled to one another. The must have figured that they had some rich American in their midst.

They didn't.

Once processed, they took me down to the jail cell. It wasn't an American jail like you see on television.

Fuck no.

This was a Bahamian jail.

The path to my cell was a dark, damp, dank hallway underneath the building with dirt floors. Wordlessly, they pushed me in my cell. It didn't have round steel bars, instead it had flat vertical slats of steel each about a quarter of an inch thick with similar horizontal slats for support.

The bars were so close together I couldn't see a thing.

There was no sunlight, no plumbing, and definitely no bed. Just these metal slats and a dirt floor and the voices from the cells saying, "Hey! Put him in here!"

I didn't want any part of that.

I had no concept of time in my 4' x 4' pitch black home. Twice a day they give me a cup of water and a rock-hard roll. A man with an English accent in the cell next to me said, "Take a sip of water and put the roll in the cup of remaining water to soften it up enough to eat."

He was right.

It was disgusting. The water was as clear as weak coffee and the roll was flavorless but I figured I had to eat something. During my processing, they didn't bother to check my pockets and I had a book of matches. Once I lit a match and saw dozens of cockroaches scurrying around me. After that, I didn't move and never lit another match again.

The corner of the cell became by toilet. I spent hours sitting in the middle of the floor with nothing on my mind except the worry of what happened to my girlfriend. I had all the money and our ID's – which were now in the hands of the police.

She had nothing.

She was alone.

It was my fault.

After two days, I was escorted out of the dirt floor cell to a small car. I had no idea what was coming next. My imagination was running wild as I'd seen way too much television to think this was going to have a happy ending. In a few minutes, I noticed a small seaplane floating on the water. Waiting there inside of the plane was my girlfriend.

Nothing looked so good in my entire life than what was before me at that very moment.

She told me she went to the U.S. Embassy in Nassau and asked for help. I have no idea how she did it or what she did – all I know is that we were heading home. A few hours later, we landed in Biscayne Bay, Florida.

We were home.

Living the life as a rock star has its consequences. I accepted that. Though the experience scared the shit out of me, I've been back to the Bahamas many times since. I often wonder if my cell is occupied by some other guy like me who was not thinking about the consequences of his actions and how they affect those you love.

Life is all about consequences and being responsible.

However, it's pretty simple. If you don't want to have to deal with consequences, then don't do anything. Just sit on your couch, stare at the wall or watch television, and wait to die.

But if you really think about it, there are consequences for inaction too.

You can't go through life, meet people, and follow your dreams without making mistakes and fucking up. You will make mistakes! We all do.

The point is learning from those mistakes and being able to move past them.

I went back to the Bahamas, but I never went to jail again. I only had to experience that once to know I was never going to get myself in that situation again!

It didn't stop me from doing drugs though.

That's a lesson whose far-reaching consequences I didn't learn until several years later.

*

Even though my time in the Bahamian jail was horrific, I learned my lesson. I never again spent another second in any jail cell.

You have to learn from the times when you've been given a second chance. If you do something stupid and dangerous and you look back and think, "I was lucky. I should have died." That's a lesson.

You don't get a second chance like that very often. Some people think they're invincible and will push the envelope. Some people do get away with it over and over again. But I guarantee it, eventually the second, third, or fourth chances come to an end and the piper has to be paid.

You will get caught.

You'll get caught by the cops and end up in jail. Or your marriage will end or you'll lose your job. Or worse yet, you'll lose yourself and your world, as you know it, will fall apart. Maybe your actions will cost you your life or the life of a loved one.

It's a fact.

The longer you get away with something and the longer you believe you won't get caught, the harder you'll fall. The worse the consequences will be. Just when you get used to your bad behavior – driving drunk, cheating on your mate, stealing from your company, whatever it is. When you get yourself to a point where the bad behavior becomes a daily habit and it becomes your way of life, the harder and further your fall will be. Eventually you will lose everything.

If you don't do right by yourself and those around you, your life will crash and burn. And the longer you get away with it, the more you'll have to lose overnight. It's happened to me and I've seen it happen to so many others.

You can never be on top forever. And if you reached the top by stepping on everyone else to get there, you will fall that much farther. When you do fall, there won't be anyone there to catch you.

I've been given a second chance and it changed me forever.

*

Now that I'm older, I understand that I have to answer for everything I do. If someone tells you that you will die tomorrow, what will you think about?

More than likely you will think of all of the bad things that have happened in your life.

"Why didn't I do this?"

"Why didn't I do that?"

"Why did I treat my wife so poorly?"

Instead of living your life with regret, live your life responsibly. I am certain that we all are held responsible for our actions – even if it's just to ourselves.

Think before you act.

Think about the consequences of everything you do and say. Prevent the regrets from even starting in the first place.

Then, when someone tells you that you are going to die tomorrow, instead of thinking about the bad, you can think about the good.

"I'm so glad I did that."

"I'm so glad I met her."

"I've lead a good life."

The good thing is that everything can be fixed – f you address it head-on. If you try to avoid your mistakes (and not take responsibility for them) the mistakes grow. They become worse. They affect more people.

Do not run.

Do not hide.

Don't do what I did.

*

I knew that taking the coke in the Bahamas was a stupid thing to do. I put my girlfriend's well-being at risk. I put my own life at risk too. But I didn't' learn my lesson for quite some time.

Most people do not come back from where I was. Most end up in the morgue as a result of a massive over-dose. I dipped my foot in the lava and luckily I had enough sense to pull it back out. I realized I had to become responsible and accept the consequences for what I had become.

I was living in Los Angeles at the time. Coke had become a major part of my life - I was on a quest for the continuous orgasm. A quest that was as fruitless as looking for the pot of gold at the end of a rainbow – it doesn't exist.

But I was determined to keep looking because that's what the first hit of coke felt like to me.

I knew that I had hit rock bottom though when I found myself alone in my house. That in itself wasn't odd – lots of people can be alone in their homes at one time or another. What was odd was the condition of my home. And me.

I was close to death, I'm sure of it.

I am certain that if I hadn't come to my senses, in a few days I would have been on a stainless steel table in the LA County morgue and some nameless person would have written my obituary.

But I was given a second chance to lead a respectful, responsible life. I had hit bottom and finally realized that I had to change. I had to crawl out of that hole I had dug for myself or die.

In my current state, I couldn't stand any noise. Every appliance, anything that made the smallest hum, the slightest noise, was unplugged.

All of my windows were closed and covered with every blanket or towel I owned. I couldn't stand the light and any breeze that came through them made too much noise. I couldn't look at the trees outside because I was certain they were really people trying to spy on me.

The day I hit rock bottom, I was sitting on my living room floor in my underwear.

Sweating.

Trembling.

It was the middle of the California summer so the house was at least ninety degrees – the air conditioner made too much noise so I had turned that off weeks before.

I had my pipe in my left hand.

I had a gun in my right.

I was shaking so badly, I couldn't hold either the pipe or the gun steady. I was barely able to focus, but I kept my concentration on the doorknob of the front door. I waited for it to turn. I was sure the CIA was going to try to take my pipe away.

And I didn't want to share.

I'm not sure how it happened, but I fell asleep. When I woke up, it was like I was looking at myself from the outside. I saw this pathetic creature lying on the floor, wasting his life. My pipe was next to my head and my gun was still in my hand.

That event changed my life.

I decided to live.

I accepted responsibility for my past, took it head on, and have never touched drugs again. I didn't go to rehab. I did everything myself.

I haven't had a single relapse.

I've just decided to live.

Now my life is nothing less than spectacular.

*

Imagine that life is an amusement park filled with all of the best roller coasters. You get to pick one to ride – each lasts five minutes. To make the ride last, you have to wear your seatbelt. Sure, the ride may be more thrilling if you don't strap yourself in, but it will be over after the first loop!

Life is like that roller coaster. Why make the ride shorter by doing stupid things!

My eulogy won't be written by some unnamed individual. I've already written it. It's gonna read:

"Thanks everyone! That was bad ass!"

CHAPTER 8

COMFORTABLE STATE OF HATRED

Be careful what you wish for, you just might get it.

Everyone has told you that in order to be truly happy, you had to get that job. To get that house. To get married. To have three kids. To have a riding lawnmower. To buy a minivan for your wife and a Range Rover for yourself. To have a housekeeper come twice a week to clean your five-bedroom, four thousand square foot home.

You've spent years getting everything everyone told you was important.

You have it.

Now what?

My guess is that you're fucking miserable.

And you know what else? The people who told you what you needed to have in order to be happy are just as miserable.

Now you are in a rut. You're stuck. Most people will stay in this self-created hole – unhappy for the rest of their lives.

Despite all of your best attempts, you are now at one of the lowest points in your life. You have fallen into what I call The Comfortable State of Hatred.

Your only hope to get out of this state is to start over.

To press the reboot button and hope to not make the same mistakes the next time. The problem with starting over is that it takes you ten years to become truly miserable – to understand that you are in the comfortable state of hatred - and five years to rebuild.

You don't need a degree in mathematics to figure out that it adds up to fifteen wasted years. Fifteen years that you will never get back – no matter how much you ask.

They're gone forever.

The solution is to not get into the comfortable state of hatred in the first place. Never become bored because once you do, you will hate your life. When you are stuck in the comfortable state of hatred, you spend more time maintaining life (the status quo) than you do progressing.

Once your life stops progressing, you stop living.

*

It sounds like a Catch 22, but life has a way of turning the tables on you when you get what you wish for. Once you start doing what you love for a career you ultimately begin to hate it.

It's true. It happens every time.

I used to love Mars bars. Remember them? I had a fan once who sent me twelve cases of Mars bars. I thought I had died and gone to heaven.

I'd received my wish.

Now I can't even stand to look at a Mars bar. I hate them. I haven't had a Mars bar in twenty years.

Life is funny that way. Be careful what you wish for because you just might get it.

*

Years ago, I had lost my job in California. I was collecting unemployment of about one thousand dollars a month and I knew exactly how long I could still make the claims and receive the money. I decided to move to Boca Raton, Florida and start over.

I set a goal for myself. Instead of being comfortable and finding an apartment for $500 a month, I rented one for $1000 a month. This way I was forced to work hard to keep it. Plus, I decided that I could always downgrade if things didn't work out.

I loved working on cars. Restoring classic cars is a passion of mine. I can look at a picture of a fender and know exactly the make, model, and year of car it came from. I'm very good at what I do. So once I found a home, I started looking for a place to open a classic car restoration business. I found a place on Delray Beach for $1500 a month. I opened the doors to my new car restoration business called Delray Vintage.

At the time, I was dating a woman I'd met in Los Angeles and who joined me in Florida. Her name was Susan and eventually became my wife. We worked together to build the business. She was great in sales and in no time had brought in a commercial account for an ambulance service. They had fifteen vehicles that we were hired to maintain. Within a week, we had five more accounts.

We were making a lot of money.

It may sound like a dream come true.

But it wasn't.

It became my personal hell.

This is what started the darkest period of my life. I'd turned my passion into my career. I was working with my mate. We saw each other twenty-four hours a day, seven days a week. Soon we had become so successful that we expanded the business and moved into a 10,000 square foot facility.

You're probably thinking, "Hey! That's great!"

But it wasn't.

What happened?

Most would think I should have been the happiest person on Earth. I had a great business. I was making a lot of money. I had a beautiful wife at my side.

The problem was that I stopped being me.

I started playing the part of someone I didn't want to be.

I put my hair up in a baseball cap, bought a new house, bought furniture, and had a daily routine. I did this for seven years. Seven years of a marriage, a job, a house, and a routine. In reality, it felt more like just one year – because I didn't progress at all in any way during that time. Sure, I progressed financially, but I had slipped into the trap - the Comfortable State of Hatred.

Let's get one thing straight. Money is great when it's meant to increase your freedom to do things and be your own boss. But when money is only used to buy material things, to maintain some lifestyle, or to show off your status, then money becomes the master. If that's the case, money has a hold on you.

I reached the point where every single day was mundane. Day after day it was the same thing. I started to hate my job. I hated my wife. I hated my house. I hated my neighbors. I hated my life.

It all became about responsibility and obligation. I had clients that relied on me and I had deadlines. I had a 10,000 square foot facility and employees who depended on me. I couldn't be myself. I should have never allowed the business to become as large as it did. I should have stayed small so that my passion of working on classic cars stayed just that – a passion and not an obligation.

You'd think being my own boss and owning my own shop and making my own hours would work for me. It should have, but instead of remaining the person I was, I allowed myself to change, to look the part of a business owner. I thought it was time for me to grow up and be a responsible adult. What I didn't realize was is that I already was a responsible adult. But somehow I convinced myself I still need to "look" like it. I was trying to fit the mold that everyone said I needed to be in order to be successful.

I started buying all kinds of antiques and cars. Whatever I wanted I bought. I'd always loved antique mechanical gadgets so I was buying everything old and mechanical that I could afford. At first, it was a small collection. Then it turned into an "I gotta have it!" kind of addiction. The stuff had a hold on me. And I didn't have a hold of myself anymore. Drugs are not the only thing a man can become addicted to.

If you have nothing tying you down, you're free to do whatever you want. Material things tie you down. If you want to collect something, collect cash. The reason most people are stuck in the comfortable state of hatred is because they have accumulated so many things.

Do you own your house? Probably not. You make payments to a mortgage company. You are obligated to them.

Do you own your car? Probably not. You make payments to a bank. You are obligated to them.

Do you have lots of "stuff"? Probably. If you had to quickly move, you couldn't because you have too much stuff to deal with. Like your home and your car, you are obligated to your "stuff."

I was miserable and I was making those around me miserable too. One day I found a note written on a McDonald's bag from my wife that read, "I'm leaving you. Bye."

She was gone.

I didn't see her for months. I was miserable and had turned to drugs to cope. It was during this time that I starting doing coke heavily. I'd been doing it since I was a teenager, but now I was doing it day and night just trying to numb myself. It was a bad time in my life. When she left, I hit rock bottom and coke became .

In the beginning, drugs were a recreational thing for me. In the beginning, drugs weren't a part of my lifestyle - they were something to do on occasion with friends. Something to enjoy when I was partying. Eventually, they became my means of coping. Once I started hating my life and who I had become I went to the one thing I knew would make me feel better.

Drugs.

Drugs don't help anything. Drugs made me hate my life even more.

Working on cars didn't excite me anymore. It used to. I loved my job in L.A – it was small and manageable. I've loved working on cars my whole life. I still do. But in Florida, I had my own shop, my own accounts, a mortgage, a wife, taxes, responsibility, obligation, and paperwork! The love of working on the cars faded. I found no joy in it anymore. I had deadlines. I had inventory.

The mundane tasks took over.

I had wished for success in rebuilding classic cars. Now I regretted that wish.

Routine and the mundane kill your spirit. It slowly eats away at your dream. It makes you forget who you are. It takes away the joy you used to have in what you did. If you spend every day just punching the clock, running errands, checking off a list, making appointments, doing the dishes, you've sunk into a comfortable state of hatred.

*

You've sunk into a comfortable state of hatred, if you wake up at the same time every day, get out of bed the same way, go through your morning routine and leave the house the same time every day. If you go through your workday talking to the same people, having the same meetings, checking off the same list, eating the same lunch, leaving the same time just to come home and lay down on the couch and watch television every night, you've sunk into a comfortable state of hatred.

It's a never ending cycle.

If you find yourself finding different ways of coping such as drinking too much, doing drugs, gambling, shopping, cheating on your spouse, neglecting your kids, you have sunk into a comfortable state of hatred.

It happens more than I'd like to say.

I see people sinking into the hole each and every day. Recently, I was talking to two investment bankers. They were co-workers at the same firm, did the same job, were the same age and had been at the company the same amount of time. Instantly, I knew one hated life while the other didn't. I wanted to see what the difference was. The one guy – John - talked about how he loved his job. He loved researching, he loved trading, and he loved making people money. The other guy – Bob - only said, "I've been doing this my whole life. It's too late to start over now."

Which investment banker would you rather work with?

Which would you want investing your money?

Let's get one thing clear. It's never too late to start over. My grandmother went to Disneyworld for the first time in her life when she was in her

80's. After that she even visited Italy and became an ordained minister! Never, say it's too late to do anything.

Interestingly, neither John nor Bob were married and neither had any children. John said he loved being single, loved living by himself. He frequented many different clubs and had a variety of interests and friends. Bob bragged about how he had real estate. When I asked him what his passion was, he couldn't answer. John was quick to say he loved numbers and math. When I asked John why he wasn't married, he said he knew years ago that marriage wasn't for him. He'd had girlfriends and he's still friends with many of them. Bob, on the other hand, wanted to be married to a supermodel.

Finally, I asked them what their biggest contribution to life was. John said he'd helped lots of people make more money and be more financially secure. John also enjoyed helping take care of some of his friend's kids financially. Bob said, "I hope it's better the second time around."

Really?

This guy was living his life only in the hopes that his next life will be better? I was shocked and saddened. What a waste.

You can get second changes *in* your life. But you don't get a second life to live. Once you're dead, you're dead forever.

It all comes down to this: find out who you are and be confident in yourself. Follow your dreams and don't remain in the past.

Change things up!

This is how you will avoid the comfortable state of hatred. If you allow yourself to stay stuck, become something you're not, lose your passion, give up on your dreams, you will sink to the comfortable state of hatred.

I guarantee it.

I believe 60% of Americans right now are in a comfortable state of hatred. I've met so many people in my life from all walks of life - different backgrounds, ages, financial situations. Most of are in a comfortable state of hatred. It's rare that I meet someone who truly was living his or her life freely and full of passion and choosing to love life every day.

That is sad. Especially when it can be avoided.

*

There's a difference between giving up and giving in. When you give in, you just allow yourself to be swallowed up by your life around you. You're punching the clock – with your job, with your relationships. You're a walking shell. And you keep telling yourself, "I'm doing what I'm supposed to do. This makes me a responsible adult. This makes me a good person. I've joined the PTA. I have a nice lawn. I recycle."

You've given in and you've lost control.

Give it a little more time and you'll find some other way to cope. You'll get a prescription for anti-depressants. You'll start drinking. You'll cheat on your mate.

I married my wife out of convenience. I bought a house, had a business, and created a routine. Fuck! It seemed like the thing to do. No pressure, just convenience. It just seemed like the thing to do next.

I've learned that most people think that way.

*

Don't get married because it's the next thing to do on the human check list. Get married when you are truly in love with someone else and they are truly in love with you. Most importantly, get married only if they've seen the real you. People can put on an act for a good year. In fact, guys can put on the act for a couple of years. Guys know what I'm talking about. Guys put on the best behavior act for at least two years. And then, it all changes. I hear it everywhere – men and women always say, "Oh they changed after a couple years." No they didn't. They weren't being totally themselves for two years! They didn't change, they just stopped the act of trying to be someone else.

Be yourself from day one.

If you're a pig, burp and fart from day one. You're going to be you eventually so you might as well just be yourself from the get go. You're going to want to be with someone who loves you for you so you should show your real self from the beginning. Trust me, the person you are meant to be with will love you as you are.

*

The comfortable state of hatred starts with complacency. You get up, you go to work, you come home, cook dinner, and watch television.

Day in and day out.

Every day it's the same thing.

Being in the comfortable state of hatred is like the instructions on bottle of shampoo: wash, rinse, repeat. Eventually you run out of shampoo.

People are afraid of change. They think to themselves, "I have this. I paid for that. I have a place to sleep. I have someone to sleep with. I have responsibilities and people depending on me." People don't want to change this because they think they've earned everything that's around them. But what have they earned? This is not living.

It's merely existing.

Change is good.

You're better off walking away from everything in your life and suffering for a year than you are putting up with this anymore. To get your life back on track for the next thirty years, sacrifice one.

It's worth it.

If you stay where you're at, you'll never truly live. You'll just continue to exist. You might as well be a bird in a birdcage. You put yourself there – there's no one else to blame. People cage themselves.

Change is great. It will get you out of your cage.

But you have to be able to accept the consequences of that change too. You have to learn not to burn bridges. You don't have to hurt people in this process. You don't have to turn away from the people in your life – that's not what I'm saying. I'm not saying quit your job, leave your wife, and abandon your kids. No. If you're married and you still want to be married, you owe it to them to say, "Look, I'm not happy. I need to make a change and I want you to do this with me."

If there is a "we" in your life, then you have to get them on board. It's your responsibility to ensure the "we" stays "we" and not just "me." If you have a family, it's not just about you. You have to put it in context of "we."

We need to make a change.

We need to start living.

We need to do something different.

Even if you're in your 40's or 50's - you still have 30-40 years left. That's a lot of years and they shouldn't be spent just existing from day to day.

Change it up.

You can do it.

*

Don't wait.

You have to recognize when you've reached the point of the comfortable state of hatred. If you're in a comfortable state of happiness, you can stop reading this book right now. But most are in a comfortable state of hatred. Be honest with yourself and take an honest look at your life. Take a real, hard, open and honest look at your life and ask yourself if this is the life you dreamed of when you were a kid.

If it isn't, you need to change it.

You need to do something different. Maybe you don't have to do an entire overhaul. Start small. Just change your daily routine. Drive a different route to work. Get some tea instead of a latte. Try a shot of bourbon instead a beer. See how these small changes feel and then start making bigger changes.

Take small steps and work into the major leaps as you gain more confidence.

*

I've been able to make many changes throughout my life. I've pressed the reboot button and started over. I've walked away from everything several times.

Live your life. Learn, create, and share each and every day. You don't have to be the big shot to be happy. Are you a chef? Do you want to open a restaurant?

Then do it!

Just don't let it change who you are. Start small and stay small. Take Sundays and Mondays off. Once you become too big, your passion becomes your master and the desire to learn, create, and share is forgotten. Once you've become so large that you are now a franchise, you're not a chef – you're a robot performing a routine day after day.

I enjoy working on my stuff again in my small, home shop.

You've probably heard or seen the movie "The Bucket List" - the one with Jack Nicholson and Morgan Freeman. Do you know what was wrong with that movie?

They only thought to make their list when they knew they were going to die.

Fuck that!

Start your bucket list at twenty.

Start it at ten!

Live your life and stay out of the comfortable state hatred. Fill your life with experiences

You won't regret it.

CHAPTER 9

POWER OF PERSISTENCE

Don't lie to promote yourself. Exaggerate.

When I want something to happen, I make it happen. But I can't do it all alone. Nobody can. You have to associate with people who have confidence in you and support your dreams and your ideas. Those people are out there – it's up to you to get out and find them.

One of my favorite places in Los Angeles was The Comedy Store. My cousin, PJ Stansbury is a Comedy Store Comic and introduced me to Dean

Gelber – the Comedy Store's General Manager. For some reason, he and I just hit it off. I think it was because we had a mutual love of cars and mechanical gadgetry. We became very good friends right off the bat and continue to be close to this day.

The Comedy Store became my second home. It became my support network. I hung out there all the time and got to know everyone who worked there. I got to know all the regular comics and all the regular customers. I still went to a lot of other places around town, but The Comedy Store was the place I felt the most celebrated and supported.

It felt like home.

When I lost my home in L.A., Dean gave me a home. It was right on Genesee and Santa Monica Boulevard. It was a really nice house and I lived there for a year. Like the good friend he was, Dean helped me. Dean fed me work and even let me use a Range Rover to get around. Without him I would have had a tough time getting through that phase of my life. He did a lot for me and helped me through a lot and I will always be grateful.

Here I am at the Comedy Store – it felt like home.

*

It was through my friendship with Dean that I learned that there is no one more persistent than a comedian. Even a bad band gets cheered. When people are drunk, they'll still applaud and cheer. A bad comedian who's bombing on stage gets silence. When you are a comedian, silence is the worst experience when you're on stage!

But they keep going. They have to learn to turn the silence into laughter.

A successful comedian knows exactly how to do that.

Why?

Comedians have learned the Power of Persistence.

They get on stage in front of these people night after night just praying for a laugh. They try their jokes out a different way. They keep going until they get that laugh from the crowd. And when they get that laugh, it's like an adrenaline rush. It boosts their confidence and they get funnier and more entertaining.

Comedians struggle big time. The Next time you're at a comedy show, laugh. Even if the joke isn't funny. The confidence boost will make them better the next time.

Talk about persistence! I have a lot of admiration for Steven Adler's persistence in life.

*

I've always been an exaggerator. I never lie, I hype. There's a big difference. When I find a place that I think is really cool, I'll hype it up on my blog. If I find a new musician that I think has some real talent, I'll tell everyone about them and how great they are. If I'm promoting something, I'll send out as much hype as the Internet will let me.

As much as I can hype up my own abilities, I'm also quick to hype up others. That's one way to get other people to support you. You can't be taking all of the time. You have to give back.

There's a difference between "a hype" and "a lie." I will hype stuff to the roof but I'll never lie. Hyping something is exaggerating to the best of something without hurting someone. Lying is hiding something to gain an advantage.

Hyping is saying, "This is the best show and you'll have the most fun on a Sunday night ever!"

Lying is saying, "Led Zeppelin will be playing live on stage tonight," and you take people's money for a show that will never happen.

I love finding new things and sharing them with others. That's my whole basis for staying in Minneapolis! I think Minneapolis has a lot of potential and has a lot of cool things to offer. I'll do whatever I can to get people to see what I see and to go where I go.

You don't have to buy into everything I say. You can disagree with me all you want. Just join me for a cocktail sometime and listen to what I have to say. Allow me to convince you.

If you're still not convinced, then be on your way. I'll never beat a dead horse. Everyone has a limit to how much they can hear. I know when to quit. As soon as people tune me out, I'm done. Usually, I'm the one tuning them out. But then again, I get bored easily.

I hosted the Paralympics' Nordic Skiing World Cup and met so many people with more persistence than I'll ever have. It was very inspirational.

Persistence is similar to struggling for your dreams. You have to keep that at the forefront of your thoughts at all times. You can't let yourself get distracted from what you want most in life. Be persistent like the comedians who torture themselves every night on stage telling jokes to a silent audience. To them, it's rehearsal. It's stage time. It's practice until they get really good and get their own special on Comedy Central. To them, the silence is worth it for the huge laughs they'll get later.

Each day in your life is stage time.

It's practice.

Learn, create, and share every day of your life.

Never give up and never quit a day too soon.

I know I'm a pest and I know I get demanding. But when I really believe in something, whether it's myself or someone else, then I won't give up until somebody else sees what I see.

This is true not only for business and making your dreams come true, but also in pursuing relationships. You have to pay attention to when it's a good time to pursue someone and when it's a good time to pull the plug.

Timing is everything.

When I was on the pursuit of my girlfriend, Nancy, I knew she was something special and I knew we'd be good together.

She wasn't so sure.

Two days after meeting her I had to go to L.A. so I asked her to go with me.

"Are you crazy? I just met you! I'm not going anywhere with you," she said.

It wasn't easy getting a mid-western, crop duster's daughter to go out with me but persistence paid off.

Okay, I have to admit, that made sense. But while I was out in L.A., I texted and called her every day. I made sure she knew I was interested and that I was serious.

Best of all, she responded every time. If she hadn't responded, or texted back with "Stop texting me, you creep!" I would have left her alone.

But she didn't.

Two weeks later when I came back, I asked her on a date and we have been together ever since. That was several years ago.

Persistence pays!

Everything I've ever done was because I had the persistence (and confidence) to back up my hype. I've met thousands of people from all over the world. Some of them have remained my close friends to this day. I just keep going to new places and meeting new people. The more people I get to know and who get to know me, the better I feel.

It's better for me, it's better for my friends, and better for the place I'm living.

It's like fishing for quality friends. You pull in the ones that are keepers and put the others back in the water. You are looking for quality people – for followers just like Jesus Christ did.

*

I went to Catholic school in my childhood so I know about the bible.

And guilt.

There is nothing more persistent than religion – it's the ultimate hype. I do believe in a man named Jesus Christ. I do believe he existed. No matter where you are in the world, there are calendars based on his life. That's just too big to be a hoax. There had to be a guy named Jesus who was born and died.

Think about it, you can't make up a story and make it take over the whole world. It couldn't happen today – it wouldn't last. The odds are that he did, in fact, exist. There are twelve different books written about the man in twelve different parts of the world. They didn't know each other when those stories were written. They certainly didn't email one another or send each other text messages.

Who knows what the real story is. Back in the day, you would have been stoned to death if you didn't believe Jesus was the son of God.

That is some serious hype!

Think of it this way: if I told you a story about a man I knew and then you tell the story to your friends and they tell their friends, by the time it gets out to hundreds or thousands of people, the story has changed! It's human nature. People make up stories every day. Stories get exaggerated and embellished. Who knows what really happened!

Nothing can be proven.

But persistence paid off.

Christianity is huge in this world and it all centers around one man.

Let's put it this way. Our calendars - our concept of time - is based on the death of this one man.

Now that's hype.

And persistence.

CHAPTER 10

POWER OF DREAMS

If you don't have dreams, you can't be living.

Throughout this book, I've tried to tell you about how important Confidence, Difference, Place, People, Finesse, Communication, Responsibility, and Persistence are in progressing in your life. Without these essential building blocks, you end up in a comfortable state of hatred.

Underlining everything though, are dreams. Too many people have stopped believing in themselves. They're stuck in that comfortable state of hatred and they are watching time (and their dreams) slip by.

It's never too late for new experiences.

*

Ever since I can remember, I wanted to be a rock star. I knew it from the moment I looked at myself in the mirror. It was all I thought about as I grew up. Eventually, I started to live the dream. I created a look. I became a rocker. I formed bands and played drums in others.

Living the rock and roll dream.

You have to believe in your dreams until they become so big in your head and so much a part of your life that you forgo everything else. I didn't go to college. I barely went to high school. I cut class every day. Only because I was given the opportunity to do work study and ultimately earn high school diploma. But if I didn't have work study, I would have dropped out. Look, not everybody is cut out to be an academic. Not everyone is cut from that cloth.

My dream and my confidence about where I wanted to go with my dream was so powerful, it overwhelmed my parents. I was so persistent that they knew nothing was going to stop me. Ultimately they built me a soundproof studio in their basement. They supported me. They believed in me because I was confident in myself and where I wanted to go in my life. I formed my first band during that time and my parents came to every show.

If you believe in your dream enough and you have the confidence in yourself to back up that dream, people will support you and help you along the way – just as my parents did.

Not everyone is going to get it – be prepared for that. Some of my relatives certainly didn't understand.

They thought I was a devil worshipper.

They warned my parents to be careful because I could eventually kill them in their sleep. I can laugh about it now, but it really hurt me back then.

Luckily, my parents didn't buy it. They didn't believe that for a second. If my mom actually believed I was worshipping the devil, she would have smacked me. After all, I'd been an altar boy.

My grandfather wanted me to cut my hair and carry a briefcase. To this day it just amazes me how much the concept of image is imbedded in our culture and of what it means to be respectful and successful. If my hair was short and I wore a tie and carried a briefcase then does that mean that I was somehow trustworthy? Would that have made me a morally decent human being?

I think of it this way. Jeffrey Dahmer, the Son of Sam, and John Wayne Gacy all had short hair. They probably carried briefcases and wore ties at times too.

Enough said.

*

If anybody says they succeeded on their own without anyone's help, they're lying. You have to give credit to those who helped you along the way. I've had plenty of help.

It's very important to have confidence and believe in your dreams so much that you get others on board with you. You have to convince them that they're getting a better deal than what you're getting back from them. You have to build yourself up enough that others will want to be a part of your dream

People like to be around passionate, confident people. They want your passion to rub off on them. They want to be a part of the action and learn from it themselves. People gravitate towards strong leaders and want to believe in them. They want to follow strength.

If you have the passion and the excitement you will succeed. It's really difficult to fail when you have the right ingredients. It's what happens after success that matters most. How you define that success makes all the difference.

If the only way you define success is by how much money you make a year, that's not passion. Money is an end result of your dream and most of the time your dream might not make you a lot of money. But I can guarantee you that you'll be happier and you won't notice what you're lacking. You'll only see how much you've progressed.

That's what counts.

Making lots of money should not be your only dream. If that's your goal, you will never make enough money to be satisfied. You'll always want more – you'll become a hamster on a wheel.

You'll be running and running and running but not getting any further in life except tired and old.

I'm passionate about music and cars. Those things are inspiring! I can continue to learn, create, and share with those two passions. Find your passions. Learn, create, share from those passions.

If your dream has the potential to make you lots of money, then great. But your dream should be the thing that you would do and would love to do regardless if you made money from it at all.

You probably hear about all of the famous musicians and how many millions they make. That's a very small percentage of the industry. Most musicians today make $17,000 a year.

That's it!

And I'm talking about the working bands who tour all over the country. They don't make a lot of money, but what they all have in common is their love of music. They love the lifestyle. They love the experiences and the people they meet. It's a shame they don't make more, but sometimes that's the price you pay to do what you really love in life.

People who have a deep seeded dream that drives them every day are excited about life. Excitement is contagious. You have to be excited about your dream and about yourself.

Once that happens, you will know what true happiness is.

Remember, when you are on your death bed, there are no do-overs for the life you have lived. At this point, your second chances are used up. When the switch is turned off, that's that.

During the 60, 70, or 80 years leading up to that switch being flipped, live your life! Learn, create, and share each and every day.

Experience life.

Start your bucket list at twenty – not sixty.

And before your eyes close, before that switch is flipped, you want your last thought to be, "Wow. That was fucking awesome."

Coming Soon From

L.A. Nik™

"Every Woman Should Read This Book" is a book for women about the male psyche. It's a book that will tell you the truth about men – how they think and why they act the way they do. It will tell you things about men that no other book will and, most of all, it will explain how to succeed in your relationship.

EVERY WOMAN SHOULD READ THIS BOOK

L.A. Nik™

Are you a fiction fan?

Check out these publications from

JOHN P.
GOETZ
The Protocol
An Eat Teague Novel

The Protocol

Your grandfather needs a new hip. **Denied.**

Your mother has dementia and requires long-term care. **Denied.**

Your son was in a car accident and needs extensive medical care. **Denied.**

You need a new knee. **Denied.**

You need an MRI. **Approved. Wait Time: 9 months.**

We live in the new United States of America. One with Death Panels. One where government-run healthcare rations treatment based on your statistical worth - in the opinion of a faceless bureaucrat.

Are you personally worth that expensive treatment your doctor has prescribed? Think again.

Aequalis Health Care, the new federally-mandated insurance provider for all Americans, has been created to control costs and pass judgment on you like an Egyptian God determining the worth of a dead Pharaoh. If your expenses can't be justified, watch out; you'll be prescribed a Protocol.

A ***protocol*** to die.

www.eatteague.com

Coming soon!

Eat Teague's 2nd Adventure

Eat's Perdition

JOHN P.
GOETZ
Souls
of
Megiddo
Book 1: The Caretakers

Souls of Megiddo

Book 1: The Caretakers

It's 75 BC and Ixzalouh's people are vanishing. He's the last Mayan High Priest. The disappearance of his people hadn't happened suddenly, but slowly over time. Only the infirm and the desperate few who don't know any better remain wandering the Mayan streets and plazas. With the help of Tepeu, his supernatural teacher, Ixzalouh creates two pendants to preserve the souls of his dying civilization. They are palm-sized granite stones each containing a hooked X on its face. One stone houses the soul, the ch'ulel, of a Mayan child named Bale'. The other stone, a mirror image of the other, contains the soul of a criminal.

In the twenty-first century, Jacob Collier is a high school history teacher who has been bequeathed one of the stones. The stone was assigned to Jacob when he was close to death as a child. Throughout his life, he learned how to understand its power and to manage the demands and responsibilities placed upon his shoulders. A secretive group called the Patrocinium helps Jacob understand the stone's history and his till-death-do-us-part role as Caretaker. Together, he and the Patrocinium must find the stone's twin and keep both from those who would abuse their power.

www.soulsofmegiddo.com

Coming soon!

Souls of Megiddo, Book 2: The Ring of Fire

About John P. Goetz

John P. Goetz is a novelist and ghost-writer. His two books, "The Protocol" and "Souls of Megiddo" have both been met with critical success and are available at all major online retailers. He currently lives in Minneapolis, Minnesota and is working on his upcoming releases for 2013.

Reviews for "The Protocol"

5 out of 5 stars

"If you love Koontz, you will love this one!"

4 out of 5 stars

"…a frightening glimpse of a possible future and should be compulsory reading for anyone."

Reviews for "Souls of Megiddo"

5 out of 5 stars

"This book will grab your attention and hold it all the way to the end."

5 out of 5 stars

"If you like to have a book grab you by your shirt, drag you into the scene and make you feel like you are part of the action, this book is for you!"

You can contact John at by visiting his blog at: johnpgoetz.com

Made in the USA
Lexington, KY
29 January 2013